EVERYTHING
is Possible

Everything Is Impossible
Copyright © 2019 Nathan Lyle Cunningham. All rights reserved.

All rights reserved. No part of this publication may be reproduced, stored in a retrieval system, or transmitted in any way by any means – electronic, mechanical, photocopy, recording, or otherwise – without the prior permissions of the copyright holder, except by reviewer who may quote brief passages in a review to be printed in magazine newspaper or by radio / TV announcement, as provided by USA copyright law. The author and the publisher will not be held responsible for any errors within the manuscript. All characters appearing in this work are fictitious. Any resemblance to real persons, living or dead, is purely coincidental. Unless otherwise indicated, all scripture quotations are taken from the King James Version of the Bible.

FIRST EDITION
Published in 2019

Author: Nathan Lyle Cunningham
www.YouTube.com/NathanLyleOfficial
www.Twitter.com/NathanLyle

ISBN: 978-0-578-57087-7

Library of Congress in Publication Data

Category: Family, Relationships, Social

Library of Congress Cataloging-in-Publication Data

Publishing Consultant & Designer: Eli Blyden | EliTheBookGuy.com

Printed & Published in the United States of America

*This book is dedicated to
every person who hasn't achieved their dream.
I hope you find something that makes your life
truly meaningful and fulfilling.*

* * *

"To live is to suffer
To survive is to find some meaning
in the suffering."
— Friedrich Nietzsche

Everything Is Impossible

Author's Note

When I originally sat down to write this book, I had no intention of changing any names. There are too many different people and it's not worth going through all that trouble just to protect their feelings. Then someone pointed out to me that changing people's names is often done in order to lessen the possibility of a lawsuit. I looked up the term defamation. I'm not a lawyer so I don't understand all the loopholes. I just know that the majority of stories in this book cannot be proven. A court case would simply come down to my word versus theirs. It's a risk that might not be worth taking. Plus, the more I think about it the less I want to say some of these names. Whether it be a positive review or a scathing criticism, there are some people that I don't want to put in the spotlight.

Everything Is Impossible

Table of Contents

Dedication iii
Author's Note v
Introduction 1

Chapter 1
   1996 7
Chapter 2
   Abuse 15
Chapter 3
   Fourth Grade 19
Chapter 4
   Friday, May 19, 2000 23
Chapter 5
   Fifth & Sixth Grade 27
Chapter 6
   Moving 33
Chapter 7
   Summer 43
Chapter 8
   Aftermath 49
Chapter 9
   8th grade 55
Chapter 10
   Freshman Year – Part 1 59

Chapter 11
My First Suicide 67

Chapter 12
Freshman Year – Part 2 71

Chapter 13
Sophomore Year 79

Chapter 14
Junior Year 87

Chapter 15
Senior Year 95

Chapter 16
Wisconsin 107

Chapter 17
Road to Haven 113

Chapter 18
Haven for Hope – Part 1 123

Chapter 19
Haven for Hope – Part 2 129

Chapter 20
San Antonio College 139

Chapter 21
Leaving Haven 143

Chapter 22
I'm An Adult? 149

Chapter 23
Things Change 157

Chapter 24
Creative Writing 167

Chapter 25
Finding a Dream 171

Chapter 26
  Student Film 177
Chapter 27
  Leaving Luke 185
Chapter 28
  Internship 191
Chapter 29
  Unemployed 195
Chapter 30
  Gwendolyn 201
Chapter 31
  2016 209
Chapter 32
  Brenda 215
Chapter 33
  The Beginning 221
Chapter 34
  Clarifications 233

  Other Books by Nathan Lyle Cunningham 245

Everything Is Impossible

EVERYTHING IS Possible

BY NATHAN LYLE CUNNINGHAM

Everything Is Impossible

Introduction

I am not a writer. Calling me a writer is an insult to real writers. I'm simply a storyteller who learned how to write so I could start sharing my stories. Learning how to cook dinner for yourself doesn't make you a chef.

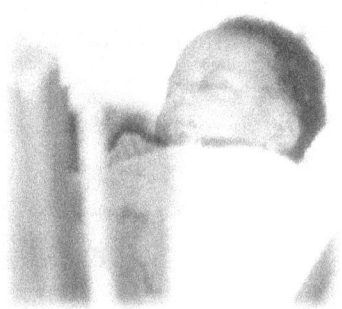

I won't be able to describe the things I heard, smelled or tasted because those things aren't embedded in my memories. I will try my best to write everything as I remember seeing it. Before you read any further you should understand that this story doesn't have a happy ending. The happiest thing about this story is the fact that it's not over yet. I'm living the sequel right now.

> "Now let's go deep inside the solitary mind of a mad man who screams in the dark"
> – Tupac Shakur. Hail Mary.

I was born May 19, 1990 in San Antonio Texas. My birth certificate says I was born at 9:30 pm. According to my mother I was eight pounds and crying like a banshee. I don't remember any of this. The earliest memory I have of my childhood was being five years old. I was in my kindergarten class when I suddenly became aware of my own existence. I knew my name was Nathan but didn't understand how I knew this. When I heard someone say this word, Nathan, I knew I was expected to respond.

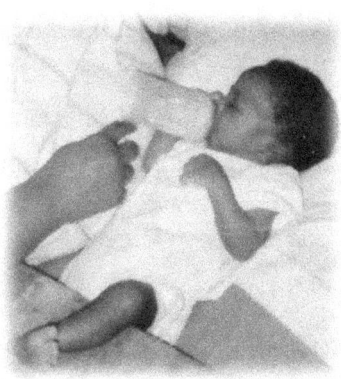

I knew that this building I stood in was known as a school. I knew that the authority figures in this building were known as teachers. I knew that when it came to naptime, I preferred to fall asleep watching The Many Adventures of Winnie the Pooh instead of Pinocchio because that creepy puppet gave me nightmares. I just couldn't wrap my head around it. How did I have five years of knowledge without the ability to remember anything beyond the last five minutes?

As my mind grasped for answers there was only one that made any logical sense. I was an alien with implanted memories. I was sent to Earth on a mission to observe this species known as humans and integrate myself into their society. It's a mission I have yet to truly accomplish. Have you seen Disney's animated Tarzan movie? One of my favorite songs from that soundtrack was Strangers Like Me. I've spent my entire life feeling that way about the people around me. I've never felt like I was one of them.

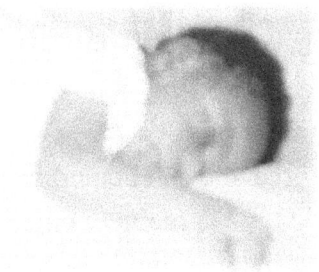

I didn't learn to tie my shoes until I was eleven yet before I entered first grade, I was already reading five hundred page novels. I taught myself to multiply and divide fractions and decimals before most of my classmates knew that one plus one equaled two. While most kids wanted to be astronauts or NBA players, I wanted to be a Nobel Prize winning geneticist with a day job as an accountant. I'd heard that scientists didn't make much money and since so much math was involved in science anyway, I figured it would be easy to do both since half of those classes probably overlapped.

My penmanship has always been atrocious. Part of the reason for that is a thought that entered my head as a young child. What happens if my hand gets cut off? I cannot recall what caused that thought to enter my head. I was likely watching a TV show or movie where a character was injured and decided I didn't want the loss of a single limb to leave me feeling completely helpless. So as I was learning to write I taught myself to do everything with my left hand first.

 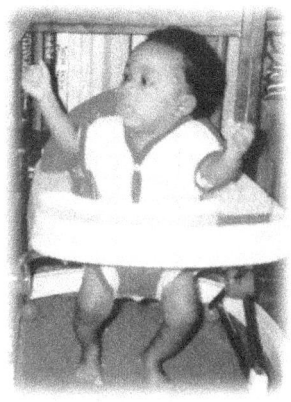

Then it occurred to me that if an accident could take one hand why couldn't it take both? What if a car crash leaves me unable to use either of my arms? So I decided to teach myself to write with my feet. I also taught myself to use utensils and turn doorknobs with my feet. I have yet to lose any limbs so those skills are nothing more than party tricks that I never get to show anyone.

The most vivid memory I have from kindergarten is a chocolate cake with blue icing and one large candle shaped like a six. The day I turned six years old my mom brought a birthday cake to the school. I should've been first in line. I wanted a corner piece. Instead we were all put in alphabetical order and I was given a side piece. They made us eat outside because they were concerned that we'd make a mess.

The moment I sat down, before I could even take a bite, the cake fell onto the grass. I cried. No matter how much I pleaded they refused to give me a replacement piece. They thought I was lying. That I was trying to scam them out of an extra piece. Just go outside and look at the grass. You'll see the piece of cake there. I hope my memories are inaccurate because that's just bull. It was my birthday and I was the only one who didn't get any cake.

CHAPTER 1

1996

Not only was I the youngest in the family, I was the only male in a household with three generations of women. My sister was nearly two years older than me. She's always been taller than me. Even right now. I'm one of the only men in my family under six feet tall. She's the only woman in the family over six feet tall. The majority of them don't get past five and a half feet. At every point in my life I would always have to tilt my head up to look my sister in the eyes. We used to be so skinny. Dangerously scrawny in fact. As we got older, we kept getting taller and our stomachs continued expanding.

My mother and grandmother are both a few inches above five feet tall. My mother has always been chubby. She blames me. She says it was easy to lose the baby weight from giving birth to my sister but she couldn't shake any of the weight she gained from carrying me. My grandmother

has been three hundred pounds my entire life. She's a shorter, rounder Madea. That's not a joke. It's not even a slight exaggeration. The first time we saw one of those movies someone turned to my grandmother and asked "did you ever babysit a boy named Tyler?"

The summer after kindergarten the four of us moved into a two-story house in the suburbs. It was a house that we had built just for us. I don't know all the specific details. I just remember being driven to an empty patch of grass and being told that we

would live there. Every now and then we'd drive by that patch and there'd be more and more there until it looked like a building.

When you walk in the front door you enter the living room. The only thing I remember was a big couch sitting across from a relatively small TV with rabbit ears on top. Next to the living room was the master bedroom that my grandmother slept in, which included a walk-in closet and full bathroom. The first floor also included a small dining room connected to a small kitchen which was connected to a small pantry where the washer and dryer were plugged in.

The second floor had a family room which was directly above the living room. There was a full bathroom and three bedrooms. One of those bedrooms had a walk-in closet. When we first moved in I slept on the couch in the family room. I attached the Sega Genesis, and later the PlayStation, to the TV in that room. After a few years I would eventually move my blankets, books and the TV into the empty bedroom.

Moving into a new neighborhood meant I was starting first grade at a new school. There are many people I met in first grade, names that will pop up in later chapters like Kyle,

Nick and Elliot, but the only one I'll take time to focus on right now is a girl named Melanie. She was the first girl I've ever had a crush on.

Well, technically I've had crushes on characters I saw on movies and TV shows like Jasmine from Aladdin or Kim from Mighty Morphin' Power Rangers. Melanie was the first girl I knew in real life who I wanted to date. Throughout my life I've been interested in girls for as little as ten minutes before I got over her. For the sake of this book I choose to define a crush as anyone I've spent a minimum of three consecutive months continually obsessing over.

Melanie had cream colored skin, long blonde hair and wore glasses. Her mouth was always very moist. I can't remember a single conversation I had with her. If not for the fact that she was my first crush I might've completely forgotten about her by now. After first grade ended I only saw her once.

My sister was in middle school and had a best friend named Priscilla. One day I was told to go to Priscilla's house to pick my sister up. I walked out my front door, turned left, walked four houses down and knocked on the door. Melanie was the one who answered. For four years she'd been just down the street and I never knew.

While I don't remember every single second of first grade there are some very clear memories that stick out in my head. One of the most impressive physical feats I've ever performed in my life was doing a handstand on top of the monkey bars. After a few seconds my arms lost all strength and I went crashing head first into the rocks. No clue what happened after that.

There are a lot of things I don't remember about first grade. I spent the rest of elementary school being told about the time I took everyone's lunchboxes and threw them across the room. It's possible they were exaggerating. Stories about me tended to balloon out of control. Like the story about the time the school called the cops on me.

I was on the monkey bars during recess when the bell rang to end the period and the teachers began gathering us up. I didn't want to stop playing. There were these gates in front of the doors. I'm assuming that after everyone leaves those gates got closed and locked to prevent people from breaking in. As I got close to the door I jumped onto those gates and scurried up as quickly as I could.

Before anyone even realized what was going on I was sitting on top of them. The teacher kept yelling at me to get down and I refused. More administrators continued to show up and I continued ignoring their orders. Then I saw squad cars pulling into the parking lot and started to worry. Would they really send me to jail over something this meaningless? I climbed down before the officers arrived at the gates.

When other people tell the story, they say I climbed onto the roof of the school and started throwing rocks at people. The cops got on the roof and chased me. I tried to run but they caught up and tackled me. In some stories I was biting and kicking the officers as they dragged me down.

There are some stories that never get told. I wonder why the fact that in first grade I would go to other first grade classes and read books out loud to them isn't talked about. My favorite kids' book to read to them was Leo the Late Bloomer. I identified with it very strongly because much like Leo I couldn't do the same things that other kids had already learned to do. I still hadn't learned to tie my shoes. I still have trouble staying in the lines when I color.

The most important memory I have of first grade is my seventh birthday party. My mother rented out a Peter Piper's Pizza for the day and I invited the entire class. No one showed up. At the time I was completely oblivious to the fact that I was such a loser. I enjoyed spending the entire day playing games and eating pizza with no concern for whether or not anyone else showed up. Then Kyle arrived. This kid was so scrawny and pale you might wonder if he's ever actually been outside. He and I played together the rest of the day. Later on we'd go to his house and play with action figures in his bedroom. That's the day we became best friends.

I don't remember too much about second and third grade so I'm going to skip over those years. Before that happens, I need to take a paragraph to talk about Spawn. I was introduced to the character in 1997 when the live action movie was released. I instantly fell in love with him. I dressed as Spawn for Halloween. I started reading the comics and watched the TV series. My uncle bought me a bunch of Spawn action figures. I created a new character that was essentially just a clone of Spawn. That character would eventually become Oscar Mireles.

Everything Is Impossible

CHAPTER 2

Abuse

As a child my grandmother appeared godlike in my eyes. Everything that happened in our household happened according to her desires. She paid the bills and cooked the meals. She bought us clothes for school and toys for Christmas. However, I feared her far more than I revered her. Throughout elementary school my sister and I were being physically abused. My grandmother used any excuse she could to hit us.

One morning I was getting dressed and didn't have any clean underwear in my dresser. I knew from experience that if I was caught wearing dirty underwear, she would hit me. I hadn't learned how to do my own laundry yet. Even if I did, I wouldn't be able to make it to the laundry room without passing through the dining room. When you factor in how long it takes to wash and dry a load of laundry and how much noise the machines make there's no way to do avoid detection. The only choice left was to not wear any underwear at all.

My grandmother was waiting for us at the bottom of the stairs. The very first thing she did was look in our pants to see if we were wearing clean underwear. When she saw that I wasn't wearing underwear she balled up her fist and punched me in the face. She yelled at me, telling me how disgusting I was. She sent me to my room, telling me not to come back down without clean underwear on. Since I had no clean underwear in my room, I just sat on my bed with my knees pulled up to my chest. I sat there for three hours before someone came to check on me.

To anyone who's ever had trouble dealing with my negative attitude…blame my grandmother. She's the reason I don't blindly respect authority figures. She abused that authority, using us to deal with her anger issues. At first I was obedient, doing all that I could to avoid the beatings. Once I realized there was nothing, I could do to prevent them my fear faded into indifference. If I'm going to be punished anyway might as well have fun breaking a few rules.

As I grew older and braver, I learned the true depths of her cruelty. We had so many beatings that I can't remember what this one was about. She grabbed the curtain rod and told me it would be twenty strikes. She didn't stop at twenty.

She kept hitting me. Forty. Sixty. Eighty. One Hundred. As she kept going her arm was getting tired and her swings started getting wild. She was just supposed to be spanking my butt but now she had moved to my back.

As she kept hitting me a thought crossed my mind. There was one thing different about this spanking. I wasn't crying. Normally when she spanked me, I would be crying by the time she finished. This time I had decided that I would take this whipping like a man and not shed a single tear. With that in mind I made some noises and forced tears out of my eyes.

My assumption was right. As soon as I started crying she stopped hitting me. I looked up and saw a smile on her face. My sister took notice of this. She started crying before my grandmother even swung. Her plan didn't work. She still got twenty swats on her butt.

Once we finished taking our punishment I went to the bathroom and checked in the mirror. I had cuts all over my back and butt. She made her only grandson cry and bleed. Then she stood there with a smile on her face. If I could travel to any one moment in time I would go to that day and call child protective services. All I would have to do is show them the cuts and I'd be free of that nightmare.

The next day when I went to school, I wore pullups under my pants. I needed extra cushioning. With my butt covered in cuts and bruises it hurt just to sit on the edge of my bed. I couldn't imagine having to spend hours sitting on those cold hard plastic chairs. I spent the entire day going out of my way to avoid drawing any attention to myself. I wouldn't say a single word unless spoken to first. I didn't play at recess. Instead I elected to just sit on the ground with my back against the wall staring down at my feet the entire time. No one said a word. I've had bad days before. They must've assumed I was just having one of my typical mood swings.

CHAPTER 3

Fourth Grade

I normally enjoyed going to school. I loved learning and could always find people to play with. I don't think too many kids actually considered me a friend. It's not hard to understand why. I was terrible. One time at recess a bunch of us were playing soccer. The ball came towards me and I instinctively reached my arms up to catch it. Remembering the rules, I pulled my arms back at the last second and let it fly past me. Kyle accused me of touching the ball. I didn't like being accused of something I didn't do. I punched Kyle in the face.

Even though I haven't talked to him in over fifteen years I still consider Kyle to be the best friend I've ever had. We went through a lot together. Fourth grade was the year everyone started having crushes. He had a crush on Karina and I had a crush on Amanda G. We told each other that in confidence and I spilled the beans on both of us. I told Amanda S who then told Amanda G. When Amanda

G asked me if it was true, I said yes. Her exact response was "ew."

I hung my head in shame. I tried to convince myself that it wasn't my fault. Maybe she just wasn't into boys yet. Then one day I heard her talking with her friends about a boy named Jordan that they all thought was cute. I decided that she was racist. She didn't like me because I was black. Turns out there were three black guys in our grade besides me. Jordan was one of them. After a while I ran out of explanations and had to admit that maybe it was just me.

My crush on Amanda G didn't last forever. I had a friend named Andrea. Skinny white girl with blonde hair that stopped at her neck. Other than Kyle she was always my favorite person to spend time with. I remember the very second that I started liking her. We were sitting across from each other at lunch. It was Friday. I never had to look at the menu to know that Friday was always pizza day.

Andrea went through the line before me and just got the first thing she saw. I didn't see the pizzas so I chose to step out of line and wait. When I sat down across from her, she immediately started begging me to trade. I told her, "If you think I'm giving you this pizza you can kiss my ass." She responded by snapping her fingers, whipping her neck and saying, "Bend Over." With no way to respond I just stared at her without blinking as I picked up the pizza and bit into it.

That was the moment I first noticed how attractive Andrea was. I never once considered telling her how I felt. If you don't include Kyle then Andrea was the best friend I had. I didn't want to do anything that could risk ruining that. Additionally, there was a classmate named John who had a huge crush on her. He confessed his love daily. She turned him down every time. Every human being on this planet could tell you John never stood a chance. Despite this, I still didn't feel right betraying him. He was never my best friend but I still liked him enough that I couldn't choose to do something that would hurt his feelings. Then came that fateful day.

We went to music class and the teacher said we were going to learn a basic slow dance. He made us line up on opposite sides of the room. The boys were told that we had to walk across the room and ask a girl if she wanted to dance. We spent the entire class sitting on the floor nervously staring across the room. John was the only one in that room to show any hint of bravery. He stood up and headed straight for Andrea. She started shaking her head before he said a single word.

John walked back to the boy wall with his head hung low. Everyone in the room was laughing at him. I turned my head to look at Andrea and we locked eyes. I smiled at her and she smiled back. I saw it all in my head. While on one knee I would hold out a hand and say, "It would be my greatest pleasure if you would give me the honor of this dance." I knew in my heart that she would say yes. I spent the rest of class trying my best not to stare at Andrea. I failed miserably.

That day might be the biggest regrets of my life. Nearly twenty years have passed and I still can't stop thinking back to that moment and wishing I'd found the courage to ask her. Sure, the possibility exist that I could've been rejected and embarrassed myself in front of the entire class. John would be angry and stop talking to me. Andrea would feel too weird around me and now I've just lost two good friends on a whim. There's also a chance that she would've said yes. Even if nothing else about my life changed the memory of us dancing together would forever remain one of the happiest moments of my life.

When I think back on my life, the many people that have come and gone, Andrea is the one that I most wish had stayed just a little bit longer. I wish I could've appreciated how special she was. Not only was she one of the most fun people to hang out with, she was also one of the most understanding people when I wasn't at my best. If I could only pick one person from my past to reunite with and talk about everything that's happened to each of us since the last time, we saw each other, I would most likely pick either her or Kyle.

CHAPTER 4

Friday, May 19, 2000

The day I turned ten years old Disney released a new movie called Dinosaur. The only present I wanted was to see that movie. I was given permission to invite two friends. Friday afternoon instead of taking the bus home I waited in front of the school with Kyle and Nick. When my mother drove up to us, I was disappointed to see my sister on the passenger side. The anger quickly faded as the three of us piled into the back seat. As my mom drove us to the theater my friends and I passed the time by singing along to the radio, much to the chagrin of my elder sibling.

We arrived at the theater just after the movie began. With plenty of time before the next showing my mom gave us some money and unleashed us on the arcade. Kyle and I started with a few games of air hockey before we moved on to Street Fighter. Then we found a batting cage in the corner of the room. A pitcher on the screen throws a ball and you swing a bat. I'm guessing the cage needed to be so big just to keep people from accidently breaking the screen. Kyle and I took turns. Whoever was in the cage would miss on every single swing while the person outside the cage would joke about how much they sucked.

As we approached the starting time for the movie my mother gathered all of us together and led our group to the concession stand. She bought me one large root beer, a box of bites size Butterfingers and one order of nachos with extra cheese. When the chips ran out, I started dipping the Butterfinger Bites into the leftover cheese. I'm the only human being I've ever known who likes combining chocolate with gooey cheese. I don't know why everyone else is so disgusted by it. It tastes amazing.

We sat in a row fairly close to the back. Sitting immediately behind us was a mother and her four-year-old son. That boy would not close his mouth. He spent the first ten minutes of the movie incessantly asking his mother questions about everything that appeared on the screen. At one point in the movie a meteor shower destroys the home of Aladar, the main character. The boy began shouting "look at all the flying rocks mommy." That was the final straw. A visibly frustrated Nick turned around in his seat and yelled at the boy "They're called meteorites! Ok kid! Meteorites!" He spent the entire meteor shower lecturing the kid.

On the one hand, I wanted to give Nick a standing ovation. The child was an unbearable nuisance. He deserved the lecture he was receiving. On the other hand, I was scanning the room for an open seat I could inhabit. I didn't want to get kicked out of the theater on my birthday because Nick made a four-year-old cry. Thankfully, neither the four-year-old nor his mother said a single word the rest of the movie.

Friday, May 19, 2000

The plan was to go straight home after the movie ended. As we headed towards the entrance, we looked through the glass doors and saw a torrential rain. My mother gave us money and sent us back into the arcade to wait out the downpour. Kyle and I returned to the batting cage hoping that one of us might eventually hit one of these pitches. Neither of us was able to figure out the trick to that game. It wasn't long before we all ran out of money and returned to the front door. The rain showed no signs of slowing. My mother instructed us to wait by the door while she went to pull the car around.

It felt like we were waiting there for hours. It might only have been a few minutes. For a ten-year-old boy with boundless energy any amount of time spent motionless is an eternity. Before long the four of us were outside playing tag in the rain. After chasing each other around for a while we started feeling cold. We searched for the nearest door, which happened to be a Sears, and ran inside.

We only took a few steps away from the door, talking and laughing as a puddle formed beneath our feet. We stayed there for a few minutes warming up, then ran right back out into the rain. We kept running around playing until my mom brought the car around. It took some convincing but she eventually got us all to climb inside.

Everything Is Impossible

Chapter 5

Fifth & Sixth Grade

The summer before fifth grade my grandmother moved out of the house. She and my mom just couldn't stop arguing. There were many different reasons but money seemed to be the main issue. My grandmother leaving was a huge adjustment. I relied on her for everything.

My mother spent the majority of her time either at work or asleep in bed. I used to wake up every day to sausage, scrambled eggs and toast. Now it's pop tarts or a bowl of cereal. The majority of my lunches were beanie weenies or Chef Boyardee. Dinner was almost always Kraft Mac & Cheese with hot dogs and peas.

My grandmother was the disciplinarian. At that point in my life the only time my mother expressed any anger toward me was when I spit in church. She said nothing so I thought I got away with it. Then we got home and she smacked me in the face. Other than that one instance she never punished me for any of my misdeeds.

The day my grandmother moved out we stopped cleaning. For two years the mess just kept piling up. By the time middle school started the floor had disappeared completely. One day I broke the faucet in the bathtub. The water wouldn't stop running and I didn't want to get in trouble. So I locked the door. No one asked any questions. We all just started using the downstairs bathroom. The faucet was running full blast twenty-four hours a day for well over a year.

I did some really stupid and dangerous things. I used to have this giant plastic toy box. I would take the lid off and put it on the ground upside down. Then I would stand on it and slide down the stairs. I liked covering the staircase in sheets so I could pretend I was snowboarding down a mountain. If I'd had blue sheets, I would've pretended I was surfing.

I lost track of how many times I did that. Not a single bruise on me. I even got my sister to try it a few times. She never got hurt. Then one day I forget to put the lid back in my room. I had taken the sheets up but left the lid at the top of the stairs. My mom stepped on it and came crashing down the stairs. She broke her leg. It was in a cast for a few months.

In fourth grade, I told the girl I liked that I had a crush on her. She responded by saying "ew" and laughing about it with her friends. In fifth grade, when I started to develop feelings for my friend Jennifer, I quickly made the decision that I would never tell her.

Every day after recess we took a class trip to the water fountain. We lined up alphabetically. She was always at the very front of the line with me right behind her. We would get our water then spend a few minutes leaning against a wall just talking. That was always my favorite time of day. There were a few times when she showed up to school wearing a fruit flavored lip balm. On those days I would spend all day thinking about what it would be like to kiss her.

One day some people came to our school with a huge tent. The entire class fit inside. We were lined up around the edges. In the middle of the floor was a machine that projected the image of stars onto the ceiling. There we are in the middle of a school day looking up at the night sky. I didn't hear a single word they said.

The only thing on my mind was Jennifer's hand. It was inches away from mine. I slid my hand across the floor hoping that when I placed mine on top of hers, she wouldn't pull away. When our fingers were nearly touching, she pulled her hand away and said "ow". Should I have mentioned that we were sitting on a carpeted floor? I was foiled by static electricity.

Fifth grade came and went in the blink of an eye. Summer passed by even faster. I soon found myself in the scary new world of middle school. The first day of school I met a skinny white boy with glasses and a bowl haircut named Blaine. We had a nearly identical class schedule. For some reason that guy just didn't like me. He said mean things to me and I retaliated.

When the school bell signaled the start of our lunch period, I hurried out the door. He approached me and flicked the back of my head. So I flicked his ear. He flicked my forehead. I flicked his glasses. This angered him. He slapped me in the face. I slapped him back. We walked through the hall slapping each other. These weren't friendly pats. Our cheeks were getting bruised.

We continued slapping each other as we proceeded down a staircase. Next thing I know I'm tumbling down the stairs. No one tried to catch me. They all stepped to the side and laughed as I rolled past them. By the time I came to a stop my glasses had fallen off. I rushed to pick them up before anyone could step on them. While most people just ignored me and kept walking by a boy named Zack that I knew from church helped me up and asked if I was alright. Then Blaine slapped me in the face as he ran by. Zack chased after him.

A few months later I had a much worse fight with two other boys. I don't even remember their names. We were in class arguing about something stupid and meaningless. When the bell rang, we stepped into the halls and I was assaulted. The bigger guy was punching me in the face while his friend kept slapping me in the back with his binder. I didn't throw a single punch. I just kept walking. They followed me down the hall and continued hitting me until I reached the stairwell.

One of my eyes was a little puffy but there was no blood. I found myself wondering why the teachers were never around when shit like this happens. Anytime I step a single toe out of line it's instant I.S.S. but on the multiple occasions when I was attacked not a single adult seemed to notice. I overheard a few of my classmates talking about the fight.

They said they felt bad for me. Well whoopty fucking doo. I don't care how you felt. You did nothing.

At the middle school I went to every student is required to take a music class. Since my voice is horrible choir was out of the question. When I looked at the brochure, I saw a piano in the orchestra section. I've always loved piano. When we contacted the orchestra, we were told the piano wasn't available. So I chose to join the band.

I walked in the door hoping to be a percussionist. The band director told me the percussion section was already full. Saxophone was my second choice. He had one on hand and told me to play it. I was terrible. The band director had the idea for me to play tuba.

He handed me the instrument and told me to play it. I blew some air into it and sound came out. It wasn't music but it was a sound. He encouraged me to play Tuba but I was more interested in the sax.

The band director told us that the school doesn't provide saxophones for student use. If I wanted to play saxophone all year my mother would have to buy or rent one. Either way it would cost thousands of dollars. There was no guarantee that I would actually commit to this instrument so my mom didn't want to spend that kind of money. Since the school provided their own tubas that's the instrument I chose.

Everything Is Impossible

CHAPTER 6

Moving

I was never going to be popular. I was born an outcast. I was beat up and picked on in every single grade. In elementary school I was too busy enjoying life to ever care what people thought of me. By the time middle school started I began to accept myself as a permanent member of the human race. Other people's opinions started affecting how I perceived myself. I was now aware of how unpopular I was. Yet no matter how much I hated the life that I had inside those walls, this was still my school.

I had a grandmother who beat me every chance she could. I shed so much blood. I cried even more tears. Yet no matter how much pain I endured inside these walls, this was still my home. There's no guarantee that my life would've been any better if I'd stayed. Yet still, I was devastated when I found out we were moving. I spent the next decade blaming every problem I had in life on the fact that we moved.

I'd spent the past five years living in a two-story house in a suburban neighborhood. Now I find myself living in a trailer park with a bedroom half the size of my old one. For the first time in my life I wasn't taking the bus to school. Our trailer was only a thirty-minute walk from the school. Fifteen minutes once I learned all the shortcuts. This was also the first time in my life I've ever worn a uniform.

Anyone who tries to tell you that uniforms lessen bullying has obviously never worn a uniform. If someone wants to make fun of you, they'll find a reason. My shirt wasn't the right shade of white. I wore my pants too high. They made fun of my belt. I never had the right shoes. If I buttoned my shirt too high the students made fun of me. If I don't button it high enough the teachers yell at me. It was a fine line I had to walk every day.

I found out very quickly that this school was far behind. Every assignment they gave me was something I'd already completed earlier that year. Academics always came easy for me but now it was literally effortless. Any paper the teachers handed me I'd just pull the exact same one out of my backpack and copy all the correct answers. There were even students who paid me to do their work for them.

Band was the only place where I wasn't up to standards. I was never going to be a Grammy winning tuba player but this group was years ahead of my skill level. In seventh grade they nearly made me repeat beginner band. The only reason I didn't is because they didn't have enough tuba players in A2.

The moment I showed up at this school the students flocked to me. They wanted to know where this knew guy belonged in their hierarchy. There was a specific group of guys that quickly accepted me as their own. I mistakenly believed they were my friends. That same group of guys spread a false rumor of me saying negative things about someone I don't even remember meeting just to get him to attack me.

That's another horrible thing about this school. The minute someone decides to fight you your life is over. If you don't fight, you're a wimp. If you fight and lose, you're a wimp. If you fight and win, they say it was a cheap shot. A week later he and his friends sneak up behind you and start slamming your head into the lockers. There were three separate occasions where I was attacked by five or more people at once. They already outnumbered me yet still felt like they needed the element of surprise. Such brave men.

Have you noticed it yet? There's a trend that will continue throughout this book. Nearly every section of my life can be marked by a crush. This year her name was Adrianna. I can't tell you why or when it happened but at some point in time, I found myself thinking about her constantly. I moved to this school in January. By the time February started she was all I could think about. When I found out that the school was having a valentine's dance, I decided to ask her out.

This was the first time in my life I've ever asked a girl on a date. I did it at the end of the school day, a week before the dance. The final bell rang and everyone was running for the doors. I sought Adrianna out. I found her just before she reached the exit. My heart was beating so fast I thought I might actually die.

Before I could finish asking her my sister approached me. After chasing her away I went back to Adrianna and barely managed to say the words out loud. To my great shock she actually said yes. That's the happiest I'd ever felt in my life. I could barely believe it. I skipped all the way home with a goofy smile on my face. As soon as I got home, I ran to the bathroom and threw up.

The day of the dance I only saw Adriana once. As I was passing her in the hallway, I asked her if we were still on for the dance. She kept saying "um. Um. Um." and walking away until she was out of sight. That concerned me a bit but I chose to ignore it.

During lunch I bought my ticket. I paid three dollars and someone wrapped a blue piece of paper around my wrist. The moment I sat down with my lunch the guys wasted no time asking who my date was. When I said it was Adrianna they got up and ran over to her. A few seconds later they ran back over to me laughing. Adrianna told them she wasn't going with me.

I was feeling a rush of emotions. Anger. Sadness. Confusion. Heartache. I stood up and walked over to her. When she saw me coming, she stood up and walked away. She wouldn't even look at me. Just kept walking in circles around the cafeteria. I kept following her, calling her name, begging her to talk to me. Eventually she got tired of running and went into the girls' bathroom.

Since that day I've spent every moment of my life wondering why. Why didn't she want to go with me? If she didn't want to go with me why did she say yes in the first place? If she did want to go what made her change her mind?

Why couldn't she tell me? Why did she run away? I get the feeling I could be ninety years old, celebrating my thirtieth wedding anniversary, watching my grandkids go to prom and I'll still be wondering what happened that day.

My heart was a wreck. There were so many thoughts and emotions filling my mind that I had trouble wrapping my head around them all. Most of all…it just hurt. It felt like thousands of sharp needles constantly flying into my stomach. On my way home I began undressing and left a trail of my belongings from the school to the trailer. My backpack. My belt. My shirt. My shoes. My sister picked it all up and returned them to me.

That day had a profound impact on the rest of my school days. I stopped taking showers after that. From February 15th 2002 to December 25th 2003 I took a total of three showers. Puberty is the worst possible time to make that choice. To make matters worse I also stopped wearing deodorant. One day I woke up to see my mother putting my deodorant on her hairy armpits. I was disgusted and made a fuss. Her response was "You never use it." Up to that point I'd been using it every single day. When I made this argument, she insisted that I show her right now. I couldn't do it. After watching her rub it on her armpits I just couldn't bring myself to touch that stick ever again.

I stopped brushing my teeth for the exact same reason. One day I walk into the bathroom to see my mother using my toothbrush. I didn't feel comfortable using it after that. What is her problem? She's the one that has a job. She has more than enough money to buy her own deodorant and toothbrush. Why are you using mine?

I don't know what happened with Adrianna but I understand why every girl since then has turned me down. I endured the majority of puberty without showering, brushing my teeth or wearing deodorant. Forget girlfriends, why did anyone talk to me?

There were many times when my mother's careless nature disrupted my life. For band we were forced to buy a t-shirt that we were required to wear at every single concert. One day I walked into her room to see her using that shirt as a rag to polish her church shoes. I shouted at her as I ripped it out of her hands. She seemed genuinely confused by my outburst. I threw it in the washing machine and it came out clean.

I was concerned that my mother might do something like that again and hid it. When the band had their next concert, I couldn't find it. I spent a few hours tearing the trailer apart and found no hint of it. Time was running out so my mother just drove me to the concert in my school uniform. When we walked in the door the concert had already begun. So we turned around and walked out the door.

I don't remember what class I had eight period but it was a source of constant frustration. There's one time when a classmate, Andre, put a pencil on the floor. He pressed his foot on it and rubbed it across the floor to make a farting noise. He blamed the sound on me. Everybody was looking at me and laughing.

He kept doing it, they kept laughing. The teacher said nothing. Yet when I hold a pencil to my crotch, she tells me I have to apologize. Andre was being much more disruptive and she pretended that it wasn't even happening. Why am I the only one who has to apologize?

I refused to apologize for actions I only took in defense of harassment. I decided entirely on principle that I would not show up to school that day. Everyone in the trailer had their own key. My mom would leave for work before I woke up. My sister would go to school early to hang out with her friends.

On a normal day I'd wake up, eat breakfast while watching TV, then get dressed and walk to school. I'd walk in the front door two or three minutes before the first class started. Skipping school required no effort. Just don't put on pants. Don't walk out the door.

The next day I woke up with a single thought in my head…what if she makes me apologize today? What about tomorrow? What if it doesn't matter how much time I miss? If I didn't show up to school for the next two years would she still make me apologize the moment I walked in the door? It just wasn't safe to return to that school at all.

I missed ten days of school in a row. That was just the first time. Later in the year I would skip school for eleven straight days. I was told that the only person who noticed I was missing was the band director. At the very least she's the only one who cared enough to start asking questions. That's the only reason word ever got back to my mother. If not for the band director deciding to ask questions there's a strong possibility I would never have returned to school.

They wanted to hold me back because I had too many absences. Thankfully my grandmother went to war with the administration. She told them that if they even thought about trying to make me repeat sixth grade, she would make sure every last one of them got fired. It's their fault in the first place. How can a kid, on two separate occasions, skip school for two weeks before anyone notices he's missing? So the absences were forgiven. As long as I passed all my classes, I'd move on to the seventh grade. Not a problem.

The coursework was always the easiest part of school. That went double for this school. Especially math. When I arrived at the school, they told me I was being placed in the advanced class. Late in the year we found out that our class was actually behind the other classes.

When a classmate asked the teacher about this, she said that she didn't think we were mature enough to handle the workload. You're telling me that you chose to turn the advanced class into the remedial class because a bunch of children were acting like children? I ought to slap the teeth out of your mouth.

Late in the year another incident happened in eighth period. The teacher left something on the projector. Class hadn't started yet so I went up to the projector to read it. Next thing I know I'm surrounded by people. They were yelling at me, pushing me. I can't remember a single thing they said. I just remember feeling so lost and hopeless.

I don't know why they're attacking me. Why does every single human at this school hate me? I was tired of this place and these people. I just wanted to go home. My real home. I wanted my backyard. My walk-in closet. I wanted to see Kyle again. I sat back down at my desk, hid my face in my arms and cried.

The story spread like wildfire. According to eyewitness testimony I was beat up by a girl named Elizabeth. When I was standing at the projector, where everyone was pushing and shoving me, I supposedly pushed Elizabeth to the ground. When I was sitting at my desk, crying my eyes out, she smacked me in the back of the head with her binder. I felt her hit me but it didn't even sting. No one in that room had realized I was already crying. It took a few minutes after class started before they began to notice. People thought I was crying because she hit me. They had no idea how much I was actually hurting.

Everything Is Impossible

CHAPTER 7

Summer

Even before I moved things had gone downhill. I only had a couple of classes with Kyle. We never saw each other outside of school and only talked a little bit during class. I was beat up and picked on. I only had three people that I'd actually consider friends. Moving didn't ruin my life. It simply took the problems I already had and amplified them.

In elementary school I enjoyed waking up in the morning. I looked forward to going to classes and learning new things. I was excited to see my friends. One year of middle school completely reversed all my feelings. I've never been happier about the start of summer.

Puberty was hitting me like a freight train. It's not an exaggeration to say I spent the majority of my free time rubbing my penis. I'm not saying this to brag. Just the opposite. It was torture. I was constantly getting erections and that was the only way I knew how to deal with them.

At this point in life I'd never had an honest discussion about sex. In fourth grade they showed us a video explaining puberty. The only thing I remember about that day was them giving me deodorant. Everything I knew about sex came from movies and television. There weren't a lot of facts.

Did you ever play house when you were a child? You and a friend pretend to be married and the stuffed animals are your children. My sister and I used to play that game all the time. Then she started middle school and some distance started growing between us.

It came as a pleasant surprise when she said she wanted to play house. We get to relive the glory days of our childhood. Then she told me that we were going to make the babies. The first thought in my head was that my cool older sister was going to teach me how to make stuffed animals.

While I could describe in great detail the events of that day I choose not to. I'll only give you the most basic information. She took me to her room. She undressed me and laid me on her bed. Then she undressed. We were together less than ten minutes. It happened twice. We took turns being on top. I felt like throwing up the entire time. I didn't understand what was happening. I just knew I never wanted to feel this way again.

I'm not angry with my sister. I'm angry at society. Why is sex seen as something taboo? It's one of the most natural instincts we have. No one told me to start masturbating. I started getting erections and my hand just found its way to my penis. Everything that happened that day could've been prevented if anyone had ever just sat us down and had an honest discussion about sex.

If there had been an open dialogue, this is what sex is and these are the things that can happen, we both would've made different decisions that day. It wasn't until a year later when I was at Mike D's trailer watching porn videos online that I realized "wait, that's what sex is? I did that last year."

I'm not saying that you should sit your five-year-old down and make them watch porn. Let's not get too ridiculous. That being said, we shouldn't go out of our way to shield them from it on the hope that your kid happens to be asexual. More than likely your child will eventually have sex multiple times with multiple partners. Talking to them about sex doesn't encourage this behavior. It simply prepares them. If your kid wants to have sex there's not much you can do to stop them. Wouldn't it be better that they're well informed and can protect themselves?

Do you realize how lucky I am that this is nothing more than a horrible memory? We didn't use any protection. At the age of twelve I could've easily gotten my fourteen-year-old sister pregnant simply because we lacked the information necessary to make a smart decision. Parents everywhere please, I beg you, talk to your kids about sex. It's only awkward because we're told that we're supposed to be uncomfortable talking about it. It's a physical activity. The only difference between basketball and sex is that one is celebrated and encouraged while the other is constantly being jeered, avoided and swept under the rug.

As horrible as that experience was it was far from the worst thing to happen to me that year. This next story requires some background information. I was raised devout. Despite being one of the most unreliable people on the planet you could always count on my mother to drag my sister and me to church every Sunday. I read the bible cover to cover. I could recite every single word by heart. Growing up the word of god was simply a fact of life.

As I was getting older, I had slowly started pulling away from the church. There have been multiple times when I spent the entire church service in the car either listening to the radio or taking a nap. Then one day I decided I just didn't feel like going to church at all.

I didn't feel like waking up before sunrise to put on a jacket and tie and listen to some guy overanalyze a book, I've had memorized for five years. I'd rather sleep late and spend the day watching football like I already lie and tell my friends I do. We could've skipped the early morning bible study. Maybe I could've worn something more business casual instead of a five-piece suit. Why couldn't she just go without me?

My mother refused to concede. That's one thing that all my relatives have in common. Every single one of us is incredibly stubborn. The more we argued the more we dug our heels in. After a while I grew tired of the yelling and ran back to my room. I locked the door and refused to come out.

I held out for as long as I could but I wasn't able to resist my bodily functions. Around three in the afternoon my bladder was ready to explode. I hadn't heard my mother's voice for a while. I unlocked my door and poked my head out. All clear. I made a mad dash for the bathroom.

I peed as quickly as I could. I didn't flush the toilet or wash my hands because I didn't want to make noise. It didn't matter. She must've been hiding around the corner. Maybe even hiding in my sister's room. She had to have been somewhere nearby, patiently waiting for me to emerge, because the moment I opened the bathroom door again I saw my mother in my doorway. She was on her knees unscrewing the knob from my door.

I yelled at her. She yelled back at me. We continued shouting at each other as she walked away with my doorknob in her hand. I stomped back into my room and slammed the door behind me. It hit the frame and swung right back open. Not only did she remove the doorknob, she also took out the latch.

I grabbed the door and slammed it three more times. It kept swinging open. I can tolerate not having a lock but now the door won't even close. What's the point of having a door at all? I took a few steps back, then charged forward at full speed.

I rammed into the door with every ounce of strength in my body. There was a big crack down the middle of the door. The hinges were bent backwards. I broke right through the frame and the door shattered a light fixture that was hanging in the hallway. There was broken glass falling down around me.

I glared at my mother to let her know that this was done purely as an act of defiance. She saw the damage I had done and her face distorted in anger. She ran at me with her arms in the air. She shoved me against the wall, wrapped her fingers around my neck and squeezed.

After a few seconds my mother released her grip and walked away. Shards of glass had dug their way into my feet. I crawled over to the bathroom to grab some toilet paper. Then I crawled back to my room, careful to avoid the broken glass.

I sat on my bed crying as I pulled the shards of glass out of my feet. It took three rolls of toilet paper to soak up all the blood. I also had blood coming out of little holes in my neck where my mother's nails had dug in. I died that day. I never stopped breathing. My heart never stopped. Yet still, I died that day.

From that moment I began questioning everything I ever knew to be true. I began to question the meaning of the word family. They're supposed to be the ones who care about you the most. Yet the ones I've always called family are the ones who made me shed the most blood. Made me shed the most tears.

Family is not about blood. Family is about the people you're closest with. The people you care most about. The ones who care the most about you. If you've built that bond of love with your relatives that's great. I don't have that love for any of the people I share DNA with. The funniest part of that story, all of this happened because my mother wouldn't let me miss church. I haven't been to a service since.

CHAPTER 8

Aftermath

Puberty is a stressful time for everyone. Your body and mind are both undergoing drastic changes. Now combine all the emotional stress that happens naturally with all the trauma I'd experienced in the past year. This led to a substantial personality shift.

A year ago, I mostly listened to Pop music, with some R&B and Rock sprinkled in. By the time seventh grade started the only thing I listened to was Hip Hop and Punk. I was growing increasingly attached to Eminem. I'd enjoyed his music before but now the words he was saying started to mean something. Especially when I heard Cleanin' Out My Closet for the first time.

When I first heard my name in the song it felt like he was signing it just for me. It greatly eased my pain to know that, as horrible as the people that raised me where, they might not be the worst parents ever to exist on the face of the earth.

> **"Keep telling yourself that you was a mom"**
> – Eminem. *Cleanin' Out My Closet.*

I'm sure a few people will try to use this to further their own personal agenda. I'm going out of my way to mention the media I consumed as a child because it was part of my development. It wasn't the sole factor in who I became.

Don't try to blame Eminem as the reason why I don't have a relationship with my relatives. Eminem didn't make me hate my mother. My mother made me hate my mother. Eminem only made me feel less guilty about it. Trying to argue otherwise would be ridiculous.

Listening to Marilyn Manson won't magically turn a well-adjusted child into a school shooter. The most it could ever do is push them over the edge. Kind of like if a guy was standing on a cliff preparing to jump when the cliff suddenly crumbles beneath him.

> **"When a dude's getting bullied and shoots up his school and they blame it on Marilyn and the heroin'**
> **Where were the parents at?"**
> – Eminem. *The Way I Am.*

Since the door was destroyed my bedroom no longer offered me any sense of privacy or comfort. I decided to move into the living room. The computer was right next to the couch. The big TV with the DVD player and PS2 attached to it was in the living room. Not to mention it was much closer to the kitchen. I took my Pokémon comforter and placed it on the couch, thereby claiming the room as my own.

I have a quick side note before you read the next paragraph. I've met so many Michaels in my life that every Michael I mention in this book will require some sort of qualifier by their name. Please stop naming your children Michael. I meet at least three people named Michael every year.

The summer after sixth grade I met Mike D. A short and skinny white boy with scraggly brown hair that lived across the street from me. I'd seen him around before. Sometimes when I was walking home from school, I'd see him getting back around the same time. Some days I could look out a window and see him playing basketball in the street. One day he knocked on the front door. When I answered he invited me out to play basketball. That's how it started. One simple gesture was the beginning of a lifelong friendship.

I began seventh grade with low expectations. I wasn't worried about making friends. I had already chosen to hate every single one of my fellow students. I was never concerned with grades. After all the trouble I caused last year I didn't skip school once this year. I only missed one day of classes after a head injury I sustained. This was the year I got my first detention. It was also the year that I stopped talking to my imaginary friends. At least out loud. I noticed people were looking at me funny and realized that everyone thought I was weird.

I made a few school friends. People that I would talk to during class about pointless stuff then forget about them completely as soon as I walked out of the building. It's quite intriguing how we became acquainted. There was another kid in my grade named Nathan. Not only did we have the same first name, our last names started with the same letter. I sat behind him in every class.

There was a weird tension between us. I don't understand why. It happened immediately and without explanation. For no reason at all we just couldn't stand each other. One day that tension bubbled over into a small fight.

We pushed each other a few times then each punched each other once in the face. Then we smiled and walked away. After that we talked every day. I know that this sounds incredibly stupid. A ridiculous cliché from an outdated sitcom. Two guys hate each other until they punch it out and become best friends. I wouldn't believe it either if I hadn't been part of it.

I don't have too many memories of seventh grade so I'll end the chapter here. Before I do, one major thing happened before I finished middle school. In 2003 Disney released The Lion King on DVD. I spent weeks going through every single special feature multiple times. One of the things I watched the most was the music video for Circle of Life performed by The Disney Channel Circle of Stars.

I saw that music video and fell in love with Hilary Duff. I'd start going over to Mike D's house to watch episodes of Lizzie McGuire. When she released her debut album, Metamorphosis, Mike's mom bought it for his little sister. The two of us listened to it much more than she did.

You might think that my infatuation with Hilary Duff isn't an important enough detail to warrant mention. Want to know why you're absolutely wrong? If it wasn't for her I might not be writing this book right now. I wanted so desperately to meet her. To make her fall in love with me. That was the first time in my life that I ever stopped to think about the future. My motives have changed as the years went by but that's where my dreams started.

> "If I could be like that I would give anything
> Just to live one day in those shoes."
> – 3 Doors Down. *Be Like That.*

Everything Is Impossible

CHAPTER 9

8th grade

My uncle never had any children. He raised my sister and I as if we were his own. There are three main reasons why he was always my favorite relative. Number one is that he never beat me. I only ever got one spanking from him. It was a single swat on the bottom and I definitely deserved it. Number two is that he's the only one who loved me more than my sister. I never felt like "the other child" when I was with him.

Most of all, his house was the fun getaway that I spent all week looking forward to. We never had cable. I had five channels to choose from and one of them was in Spanish. Not only did he have cable, he was the first one in our clan to buy a DVD player. Every gaming system I've ever owned was given to me by my uncle. He worked hard to mold me in his image.

My uncle instilled within me a love of everything superhero related. He had an impressive comic book collection. He worked at a comic book store. Sometimes he had to work on a day he was watching me. I'd spend the entire day hiding behind the counter reading comic books.

When he moved away, he sat down with me and had a long talk about why. Overall the message is that he just wasn't happy here. He was moving to Wisconsin to live with his childhood best friend. I felt like I was being abandoned. He was running away when I needed him most. The more time that passed the more he felt like a stranger to me.

On the first day of eighth grade I met a girl named Valerie. She was in six of my eight classes. She was a few inches shorter than me with skin so pale that I wouldn't be shocked if you told me she's never seen sunlight before. She also had braces and long black hair, both of which she would get rid of later that year. Well, she got rid of her braces completely but she only cut off half of her hair.

I never got the chance to really know her. The one thing I can say about her that I couldn't say about anyone else is that she wasn't mean to me. At least not to my face. She didn't go out of her way to avoid me or insult me. I barely ever said anything to her and she barely ever said anything to me. The only thing that came of my one-sided crush is that my interest in her snapped me back to reality.

When we went on Christmas break in December I started showering again. I wanted to smell good for her. Unfortunately, by the point in time our bathroom had grown so filthy that even I was too disgusted to step inside. My sister had chosen to move in with my grandmother.

Not sure how my mother kept clean, if she even bothered to try. I began showering in the same place that I pooped…in the grass behind the trailer. I would fill two empty two liter soda bottles with warm water. Wet myself with one, rub myself down with soap then rinse off with the other.

For the last six weeks of the school year I was grouped with Valerie in math class. On the last day of school, I asked her to sign my yearbook. She wrote "thanks for all the help in math." When I read that I couldn't help but laugh at myself. I'd spent the entire year in love with her and that's the only thing she could think to write. That, in a nutshell, is the story of my life.

I was normally excited for the end of the year. I hated this school. I was happy I'd never have to see this building, and half of these people, ever again. This time was different. I was scared stiff. I was going to be starting high school. I'd be joining the marching band. I was going to start dating. I was moving another step closer to adulthood. Soon after would come college, jobs, marriage and kids. Then I'd get old and die.

While I was writing this section, I took the time to look up the term midlife crisis. One definition describes a midlife crisis as "a psychological crisis brought about by events that highlight a person's growing age, inevitable mortality, and possibly shortcomings of accomplishments in life. This may produce feelings of depression, remorse, and anxiety." That has happened to me seven times.

Every single one of my teachers was making such a huge deal out of it. My science teacher went one by one telling every kid in the room how special she thought each of them was. I hid under the table so she did me the favor of skipping me. I've never felt comfortable being praised. I guess my self-image issues run very deep.

A couple of the teachers cried as they said goodbye. A couple of them made sure to hug every single child. I spent two and a half years hating that place every single day. I never thought it would be so hard to leave. It felt so weird walking out those doors knowing I'd never be back.

In our final period that day the teachers turned on the TV. It was a music channel. Can't remember the specific one. Most likely MTV or BET. The last video we watched was All Falls Down by Kanye West. It was playing as the final minutes of our middle school lives ticked away. When the bell rang, we all burst through the doors and ran through the hallways shouting joyously.

As soon as I was out of sight of the others my smile disappeared. I went to Mike D's trailer to hang out for a few hours. I didn't want to be alone. I knew that if I was left by myself, I wouldn't be able to stop the tears. Do you remember a song by Usher titled Burn? It was the biggest song on the radio. Mike helped me rewrite the lyrics to say goodbye to our former school.

> "We've been coming here too long.
> It's been 3 long years, 6 semesters,
> I'm going to miss Anson Jones."

CHAPTER 10

Freshman Year – Part 1

The summer before I started high school, we moved a couple of blocks down the street into a two-bedroom apartment. Slightly smaller, slightly cheaper. This was too much change for me to handle. Living in a new apartment, about to go to a new school with thousands of new faces. The last time I started a new school I was put through hell.

A girl from middle school wrote down her phone number when she signed my yearbook. She told me to call if I needed anything. Based on her reaction when she answered the phone, I don't think she ever expected to actually hear from me. I didn't expect to call her either. I'm glad I did. As it turns out, she was as nervous as I was about starting high school. It eased my mind to know that there were others struggling with these same feelings.

For me and three hundred other students high school started three months early when we showed up for band camp. I was not looking forward to it. I only chose to stay in band for high school because it meant I wouldn't have to take gym class. The most important thing to know about marching band is that summer in Texas always get above one hundred degrees Fahrenheit. If you're not used to it that kind of heat can literally kill you.

I definitely was not used to spending hours at a time stomping around a football field in that intense heat. Every day I went home so exhausted I could barely stand. The mental fatigue was even worse. There was so much to learn.

So many rules, so many songs. I was honestly hoping that I would suck so much that they'd make me an alternate. We had over three hundred band members. There were alternates in almost every section. Unfortunately, tuba was one of the sections that didn't have enough people. We had to move people from other sections so we could fill out the formation better.

Once band began, I found myself in a microcosm of the overall high school experience. Surrounded by hundreds of strangers I desperately clung to whatever familiar faces I could find. Other than my fellow tuba players I basically only talked to Chris and Joe. I knew both of them from middle school.

Joe was tall and skinny with a slight tan. He's that guy you see in so many movies. Looks like a total nerd but turns out to be a martial arts master. Chris was a Puerto Rican teen from a military family. They moved around a lot and he ended up getting held back a couple of years. When a sixteen-year-old with a mustache showed up in eighth grade it drew a lot of attention. A barely talked to him at all that year. Then high school started and we instantly became best friends.

When the school year officially began, I was relieved to find that Chris and Mike D were in most of my classes. Science was the only class I took that year where I didn't have a single one of my middle school friends. That was the last year that the school used the A/B class schedule. We had four classes each day. They all lasted an hour and a half. Every single class felt like it dragged on forever. Then three days a week the endless monotony of school is capped off with a two-hour band practice.

On my very first day of school I met a girl in U.S. History. Short white girl with blonde hair, blue eyes, crooked teeth and freckles. I won't say her name. There's no point. I'm going to skip ahead to the ending. One day, Chris and I went to grab our lunches. As we were stepping out of line she shouted and waved us over. When we sat down next to her, she asked us our names. Let me repeat that. She asked us our names.

Do you have any idea how much that hurt? I sat next to her every day for three months. I asked her out twice. Yet here she is asking our names. She only recognized us as the two guys from history class. Not much of a feat considering we're two of the most recognizable people in the room. I was the only black guy and Chris was the only one with any facial hair. Have you ever listened to a song called True by Ryan Cabrera? That song perfectly describes how I've felt about every girl I had a crush on in high school.

> "Do you see me too?
> Do you even know you met me?"
>
> – Ryan Cabrera. *True.*

I want to clear up some misconceptions about high school football in Texas. I've seen too many movies and TV shows where it is the center of the universe. That mostly applies to small towns with populations of only a few thousand where there's literally nothing else to do on a Friday night.

San Antonio has over a million people. Unless you're in high school with friends on the team, or you're a parent with a kid on the team, you can probably find better ways to spend your free time. I spent four years going to nearly every single game and can't name a single quarterback we had. Every player I can name is someone I either had for a class or have known since middle school.

Many people in marching band hated football. They have other things they'd rather be doing. The band directors hated that we had to take time out of our week to learn stand tunes. They'd much rather spend that time preparing us for the UIL marching competition. The only positive thing about going to the games is the halftime performance. It gave us the opportunity to do a run through of our UIL routine. They'd record it and on Monday we see the video and get yelled at for everything we did wrong.

Fridays for me were eighteen hours of pure hell. I had to wake up early to get to the band hall. There was a uniform, blue jeans and the band polo they forced everyone to buy, which we were required to wear for the entire school day. The band would assemble and take time to warm up. Then we'd march single file into the courtyard with the percussion playing a cadence. That courtyard starts feeling pretty small once the entire student body is crammed in there. The best thing about those pep rallies is that they eventually ended.

After enduring another torturous day of useless public-school education, we all had a limited period of time to eat dinner before we had to get ready for the game. There were many people who ran out the door as soon as the final bell rang. Some ran across the street to grab tacos. Some ran to the corner store. Some ran to Church's to grab chicken strips.

The day of my first ever game my mother brought me an Italian foot long from Subway. I ate outside, a foot away from the front door, because I was told no food was allowed in the band hall. When I finished eating, I walked into the instrument room to see half the brass section stuffing their face with pizza. Turns out they had a game day ritual.

Every Friday they would sneak pizza into the instrument room and stand around stuffing their faces. When the pizza was gone, they'd move a ceiling tile and throw the empty boxes up there. Once they were done eating, they'd clear the middle of the room, stand in a circle and watch two guys punch each other. It was normally very civil. No punching allowed below the waist or above the neck.

There was one time I broke this rule. I was boxing my section leader AJ and he had me in a headlock. I was trying to punch his stomach but my hand went a little too low. He got pissed, threw me to the ground and started stepping on me. A few times on my abdomen then finished by stepping on my penis. Have you ever had a 300-pound man step on your penis? That's a pain I could never forget.

If you weren't aware of this before that last paragraph should make it painfully obvious that the majority of brass players were males. The tuba, baritone and trombone sections were especially a sausage fest. The French horns section was the one place where there were more girls than boys. Every year there was only one male French horn player and he always got picked on.

The bus rides to and from, as well as sitting in the bleachers at the game, were about what you'd expect from teenage boys. We spent more time watching the cheerleaders than we did the game. One thing that really stuck out was the hydration situation. I learned quickly how important it was to fill up on moisture before we left for the game. The only thing provided by the band was a single cup of water after the halftime performance.

The water issue was just one of the many things that made band really difficult. There were plenty of times when I struggled. There was one time when we were getting really close to UIL. We already went through a full afternoon of practice and the band directors wanted to close out with a run through.

For those who have never been in marching band here's how it works. A full show is usually around eight minutes.

We spend eight minutes stomping around a football field in ninety-degree weather while playing music the entire time. The first run through was about as perfect as you can expect high school students to get. The band directors still wanted us to run through it one more time just to be sure.

As we were getting to our opening spot, I was telling AJ that I felt weak and didn't think I could make it through. He told me that it would only be one more run through so try to tough it out. I said I would do my best.

For the most part everything was okay. Then we reached the third movement. There was a set halfway through where we were moving backwards. Andre and I were both moving over twenty yards and we had to do it in eight steps. We were basically jumping backwards on our tiptoes.

We reach that set and suddenly all I can see is the sky. I'm wondering why everything is so blue...then I see the sousaphone flying in front of me. Once I realized what was happening, I barely had time to think "oh shit!" before I hit the ground. Then the sousaphone hit me. A thirty-five-pound hunk of metal landed right on my shoulder. It was unbearably painful. Thankfully there were no broken bones.

Schroeder helped me up and guided me to the sideline before rejoining the formation. I just sat there rubbing my shoulder while I watched them finish. The story they tell deviated from reality. They say I tripped. Nope. I fainted from exhaustion. My body was too worn out and couldn't keep going. They said I threw the sousaphone off. Nope. It slid off on its own.

Everything Is Impossible

CHAPTER 11

My First Suicide

Throughout my life there are times when I've wondered if I had some sort of mystical powers. I had multiple prophetic dreams. Once in elementary school I had a dream that I was Pinocchio standing on stage singing I've got No Strings. The next day a ventriloquist comes to the school and invites me on stage to be part of the act. Once in middle school I woke up and went to class. It was a normal day at school until fourth period. We had a foreign substitute with a name I absolutely could not pronounce and won't even bother attempting to try and spell.

Halfway through fourth period the bell starts ringing. I was excited to get an early lunch until I realized that it wasn't the school bell. It was my alarm clock. I hadn't even realized I was asleep. I woke up and went to school. For the first four periods thing happened exactly like they had in my dreams. The same exact conversations with the exact same people. The exact same substitute in fourth period with an unpronounceable name.

Freshman year of high school I had a strange dream. I was walking alone through a corridor. It stretched so far that I couldn't see the beginning or end. There were doors lined up on either wall. I fearfully walked through the hall concerned that any door I opened might be hiding a black hole. I stepped to one door and heard music. When I opened the door, I saw some kid, scrawny and pale with glasses and floppy hair, sitting in front of a black grand piano.

He motions at me, beckoning me to sit next to him on the bench. I was hesitant at first but made my way to his side. Once I was seated, he began playing. It's been so long since I heard it that I no longer remember the melody. Even at the time I couldn't have told you what song he was playing. I just remember sitting silently, watching in awe as his fingers moved across the keys. I closed my eyes and let the music caress my ears.

When he finished playing, he turned to me. He smiled, nodded his head, then stood up and walked out of the room closing the door behind him. I turned to the piano and tried to see if I could copy the music, I just heard him play. When I pressed the keys, no sound came out. I stood up and ran out of the room. I searched the hall but saw no sign of him. All the doors had disappeared. Even the one I just walked through.

The next day I arrived at the band hall and heard some shocking news. A student killed himself. When they said his name, I didn't recognize it. I was filled with dread when I saw a picture of him. This was the guy from my dream. From what I understand he was already dead by the time I fell asleep. Did a ghost invade my dreams? Was he trying to tell me something? Was there a message he wanted me to give to someone?

As the day went on, I kept seeing pain everywhere. The halls were flooded with tears. It seemed like every person in the school was crying for him. If I'm being completely honest, I really didn't care that he died. I didn't know him. I've never had a single conversation with the guy. He's just another student that I passed in the halls.

Still, I spent the entire day holding back tears. There was a single thought that kept running through my head. Nobody would cry for me. My relatives would attend my funeral only out of obligation. No one would miss me when I died. The world would keep spinning. Life would go on as if I never existed.

One week later, on a day we didn't have practice, I tried to kill myself. I got home from school sometime around four and went straight to my room. I wrapped a belt around my neck and put it through the buckle. I took the end of it and wrapped it around that pole in the closet where you hang the clothes from. I let my body go limp. My nose started to drip blood before I lost consciousness.

I'm not sure how close to death I actually was. There was no bright light. No life flashing before my eyes. There was only darkness. Other than a slight bit of discomfort in my neck it was just like going to sleep. Then I opened my eyes. I was laying on the floor. I hadn't tied the knot well enough. It came undone. I looked at the clock and it was almost 6:30. I went to the bathroom and washed my face. My mom got home just as I was walking out of the bathroom. No one ever found out what I tried to do that day.

I once overheard two guys having a conversation. One of them said, "I would never have the courage to do something like that." I wanted to tell them they were wrong. That it takes more courage to fear death than it does to embrace it.

Five for Fighting has a song called 100 Years. Listening to that song always makes me sad. He talks about all these milestones of life. Milestones that I know I'll never experience. When I hear those words, I think back on how horrible the first fourteen years of my life were. I can't help but think, "I can't take another eighty years of this." I tried to kill myself every single year of high school.

> "At 15 there's never a wish better than this
> when you've only got 100 years to live"
> — Five for Fighting. *100 Years.*

CHAPTER 12

Freshman Year – Part 2

I decided to rededicate myself to the band. I wanted to be the best. I wanted to win marcher of the week. I wanted to get first chair. I wanted the tubas to always win section of the week. I wanted to get that one at UIL then go on to win state. I worked harder than ever before…for about a week.

There's something I learned as an adult that I wish I could've realized back then. I never had the passion or love needed to excel in marching band. I focused on being the best for a short time because I wanted a goal to work towards. I never cared enough about the tuba to ever actually be great.

In the seven years that I played the tuba I practiced at home a total of three times. There were people in band who would practice three times a day outside of the required practices. I wish I had been aware of that massive difference in effort. At the time I just assumed that I couldn't catch up because I just wasn't good enough. That, along with constantly being rejected by every girl I've ever had feelings for, were key factors to me developing an inferiority complex that still follows me to this day.

When marching season ended my life became relatively boring. The majority of the time when the school day ended I would either go straight home to play video games or I would follow Mike D back to his trailer. Most often we would play video games or shoot some hoops. He would always beat me.

I always thought that I just had no natural talent. Once again, I now realize as an adult that it came down to effort. He played every day. Even when there was no one else around he'd still go out there every day to practice dribbling and shooting. He never once made a school team but he never stopped loving the game.

How should I describe my life as a high school student? I was a band geek but that wasn't a negative thing at our school. The band had more trophies than every sports team combined. Within the band finding your clique was easy. Most people were arranged by year and section. Most of my band friends were tuba players and freshman in other sections. Outside of the band I didn't have a clearly defined place.

I was always adjacent. I've been on the football field playing with guys actually on the team. I played card games with the nerds. I've skipped school like the rebels. The only things I never took part in were drugs, alcohol and sex. My main group of friends were people like me. We weren't big enough losers to be made fun of but not popular enough to give a damn about. You know how in movies they hire people to stand in the background and fill out the scene? That was us. We were the extras.

I never cared about popularity. I never got upset when people spread rumors about me. In middle school I had more important things to worry about. I moved to a new school where everyone beat me up or made fun of me. My sister raped me and my mother tried to kill me. I was too traumatized to worry about preteen drama. I put up a very thick wall. In high school once the desire to socialize returned I was already an outcast.

I had developed the mindset that I was invisible. I assumed no one noticed me. I assumed that people forgot about me as soon as I left the room. So whenever I heard a rumor about myself I was pleasantly surprised. You actually think about me when I'm not around? You actually care enough about me to make up these ridiculous stories and spread them around? Wow! It's nice to know I'm that important to you!

When the second semester came around Chris started dating a trombone player named Elise. She was tall and skinny with long blonde hair and a permanent glare stuck on her face. I never liked Elise. I was shocked when Chris brought her into the group. Worse still, it wasn't just one new face. Elise brought her best friend Jamie with her. Jamie, like Elise, was tall with blonde hair. Jamie's skin was much lighter than Elise's and her hair was curly. She also had glasses and braces.

When Jamie first showed up I didn't want to accept her as part of our group. Everything changed on February 14, 2005. I had planned on skipping school that day. I was lonely and miserable and couldn't stomach thought of being surrounded by all the faux romance. After lunch I was sitting in class with Chris. During our conversation he let it slip that Jamie, who missed school that day due to illness, had a crush on me.

Being the desperate, lonely and horny teenager, I was, there was only one choice to make…fall in love with her. When she returned to school the next day, I wasted no time asking her out. She said no. It caught me off guard but I was determined to see this through. After school I walked her to the buses. I asked her out again. This time she said yes. For the first time in my life I finally had a girlfriend.

Our relationship started off slow and simple. After classes ended, we would meet in the hallways and talk as we walked. We'd sit together at lunch. After school I'd call her on the phone and we'd talk for two or three hours. We were together for a week before we actually started holding hands and kissing. The kisses started as just a peck on the lips as we said hello or goodbye. After a few weeks we'd be making out during lunch.

For nearly a month my life was perfect. Then we went on spring break. Her family went on vacation so we didn't see or talk to each other for ten days. When we returned to school, we picked up right where we left off. Everything was going fine. Then she had to ruin it. There's one thing that's always bothered me about Jamie…she was a Pacers fan.

Her family was from Indiana and the team still had Reggie Miller back then so I could tolerate her devotion. I could not tolerate her badmouthing my Spurs. We were having a perfectly lovely day when out of nowhere she just randomly decides to say, "I saw the game yesterday and the Spurs sucked." How dare she! They played without Tim and Manu and still managed to beat the Rockets. Tony hit a teardrop right over Yao Ming's outstretched hands.

I fought back. She insulted my team so I insulted hers. She insulted Tony and Manu so I insulted Steven Jackson and Ron Artest. Then…she did the unthinkable. She insulted Tim Duncan!

There are some lines that you just do not cross! I would never say a negative thing about Reggie Miller! I told her to get out of my sight. I had nothing to say to her. By the end of the week, on April first of all days, she broke up with me. The Spurs won the championship that year and two more since. Meanwhile, the Pacers haven't even been able to get to the finals. Therefore, I feel like I did the right thing.

Then again, the only girlfriend I've ever had in my life dumped me. The story made it around the school that we broke up because of basketball. Some people called me an idiot. A few called me a hero. The truth is, that argument had nothing to do with our breakup. It was just the catalyst. At the core of it all neither of us really thought the relationship was worth fighting for. She chose to break up with me. When she did, I wasn't sad at all. Then something happened that would change my life forever.

A week after Jamie dumped me, I was headed to lunch when I saw her in the courtyard making out with some guy that looked like Fred Dukes. For those of you who have never read x-men comics, Fred Dukes is the birth name of the character known as The Blob. I know this guy's real name. I could even link you to his Facebook page. For the sake of my own ego I'm just going to keep calling him Blob.

One of my greatest strengths in life is the ability to overanalyze everything. Many thoughts were surging through my mind. We were together over a month before she felt that comfortable with me. Did she start seeing him while we were still together? Is that the real reason she broke up with me? Was she cheating on him with me? Did they break up and she only used me to make him jealous to get him to come crawling back? When she said she was on vacation during spring break was she really just sneaking over to his place and fucking his brains out all day?

After millions of thoughts had passed through my head I settled on the most logical conclusion. It was me. I was just that disgusting. She never liked kissing me. It was a chore that she forced herself to do. She had to ease her way into it. Once she got used to it, she could kiss me without throwing up but she never enjoyed doing it.

The worst part about the experience is that Jamie kept trying to be my friend. You just dumped me. Why would I want you showing up with your new boyfriend? Seeing them together really hammered home the idea that I was going to die alone. I blew my only chance at love. I chased away the only female on this planet that would ever want to be with me.

Then one night I was watching TV and saw an episode of Reba. I had a newly developing crush on Scarlett Pomers. I can't remember if this was the episode where she kept playing her guitar all around the house making up funny songs to annoy people, or if she was already in a rock group and they were participating in some sort of battle of the bands thingy. Either way, an idea popped into my head. I've always heard that chicks dig guys that can write songs. So I decided to win back my ex. That night I pulled out a pen and an empty notebook and wrote Jamie a love song.

That's how my journey started. One attempt at a song. Some people might hate me for saying this but it was pretty easy. I figured songs are just poems performed with instruments. I'd been into poetry for years so that was an easy transition for me. Write a poem while imagining instruments in the background.

I wrote a song and gave it to Jamie. She accepted it. So I wrote another one. Then another one. Then came the legendary weekend when I wrote ten songs in two days. She didn't accept those. When I pulled out that big bundle of paper, she told me to stop and that I needed to get over her. That should've been my first clue to a fact that would take years for me to realize. Girls like when a guy writes a song about them. Writing a song won't make a girl fall in love with you.

CHAPTER 13

Sophomore Year

When I initially started writing songs it was a misguided attempt to win back the affections of a girl I never cared much about anyway. I ended up discovering something that would become a life-long love. Every song I wrote was about the pain I felt in this lonely life I lived. The longing for a love I'd never find. I wrote what I knew. Mostly sticking to Hip Hop and R&B with a little bit of pop sprinkled around in there.

I was so wrapped up in my new obsession that I honestly can't remember anything that happened the last two months of the school year. I passed every class and can only assume that the early summer days were spent mostly staying up late, sleeping in, and playing videos games. I probably hung out with Mike D a few times as well.

I spent the month of July staying in Wisconsin with my uncle. Most of my time was spent playing video games. Kingdom Hearts 2 was slated to be released soon so I made sure to play through the original Kingdom Hearts as well as Chain of Memories. My uncle and his friends went bowling every week and always forced me to come along.

The best part about that was the deep-fried cheese curds. Those things need to exist in every building in the world.

The day after I got back to San Antonio, I went to band camp. After my freshman experience I was planning to quit. Then I found out both of the band directors were leaving to take on different jobs. I decided to stick around and give the new directors, Foster and Lozano, a chance. Maybe it would be better with them. It couldn't possibly be worse.

I arrived at the start of the second week. I expected to be too far behind to catch up. Luckily, these new directors weren't slave drivers like their predecessors. An entire week gone by and the band hadn't even stepped outside yet. They led us through slow and steady. They made band feel less like the military and more like a family.

The biggest downside to the new regime was the lack of success. Our performances weren't as polished and precise. We only got a two at UIL. It was disappointing. Freshman year I experienced plenty of success with minimal effort. I worked much harder this year. It hurt to know that it wasn't good enough. At least for now I still had an excuse. I had yet to give one hundred percent. I could work harder next year. It must've hurt much more for those people who did give it their all. Especially those seniors who would never get another shot at it.

The band was less successful but far more fun. I reached a point where I actually looked forward to going to the band hall every day. It became my favorite place in the entire school. I accidently helped start a tradition. When Christmas was approaching, the band directors invited all the students to stay after school and decorate the band hall. Only a handful of us showed up. We decorated a tree and the walls a little bit. A few of us came up with the idea that the band could do secret Santa and we'd have a Christmas party where we trade gifts. Lozano loved the idea.

So that's what we did. Anyone who wanted to participate would sign up. I signed up but never really figured out what to do so I just created a homemade card and put a twenty-dollar bill inside. The day of the party I hung out with the members of my section. There was some eating, dancing and simply hanging out. It's the first party I went to in high school. It was fun. I wish I had more memories like that. I've been to three dances in my entire school life and all of them were thrown by the band.

At the end of the year the band directors and boosters put together a banquet to thank everyone for a year of hard work. Unlike the Christmas party where everyone showed up exactly how we dressed on a normal school day the banquet was a formal event. We had to pay to get in and we were expected to dress nice.

My grandmother went shopping with me and we bought a five-hundred-dollar suit. We didn't pay five hundred dollars. It was on sale for one hundred. I just want to make sure you know that this suit was worth five hundred dollars. I wore it one time and since then it's spent more than a decade hanging in a closet encased in its bag.

The banquet was exciting. There was a ton of great food to fill up on which was the main reason I went. There was also dancing. I spent most of the night hanging with my section member Deshay. He and his freshman buddies would become the crew I spent the most time with for the remainder of my school years. I remember the entire group dancing together to songs like Dirty Little Secret and Grillz.

There were also some slow dances. One of which I danced with Jamie. If I remember correctly, she came as Elise's guest. The other two dances were with a girl whose name I cannot recall. She went to a different high school from us so it was

someone that somebody knew from middle school. For once in my life I didn't feel nervous talking to a cute girl because I knew I'd never see her again.

My second suicide attempt was doomed to fail from the start. I kept hearing that it was impossible for a human to drown themselves. I wanted to prove them wrong. They were very right. First I filled the bathtub with water and just laid in it. I couldn't stop myself from popping back up.

I thought of combining drowning with other methods. I took all the ice in our freezer and dumped it in the water. We only had one tray of ice cubes so it didn't do much. Hanging myself almost worked last year. So why not hang myself and drown myself at the same time? That didn't work either.

My third attempt happened months later. I took a steak knife to my room planning to cut myself. I put a towel down on the floor and sat on it. I didn't want to leave any evidence in the event that it didn't work. There's just one thing I hadn't calculated. I was afraid of needles. I've never been able to get a shot from the doctor without wanting to cry.

You're probably thinking the same thing I did back then. Needles and knives are two very different things. As it turns out, I just don't like sharp objects. I can't handle the feeling of something cutting through my skin. I spent hours crying as I held the knife to my wrist. Eventually I just gave up. I threw the towel in the dirty laundry and put the knife back in the kitchen.

Sophomore year was a period of growth for me as a human. I was becoming more aware of the people around me. There was a girl named Summer who I considered the definition of pure evil. Neither of us has ever had a single nice thing to say about each other.

One day I saw her arguing with a classmate. He said something to her then walked away. She started crying. I didn't know how to feel. I couldn't stop staring at her. The moment I saw her tears was the first time I saw her as anything but a heinous hell spawn. I never made fun of her again.

From that moment on I was consciously aware that these people around me are all humans. We're all doing the best we can to make the happiest life we can for ourselves. Most people don't wake up in the morning thinking "I wonder what I can do to make Nathan's life miserable today." Everyone has aspirations and fears. Knowing that, I have trouble ever choosing to be mean to someone. I try not to hate anybody. That's more difficult for some people than with others.

Sophomore year I began to question my sexuality. I considered myself bi-curious for the next two and a half years. I never once questioned whether or not I like girls. I've always loved females. I only started to question because so many people kept calling me gay or fag. I thought maybe they knew something I didn't. There are plenty of men that I can admit are attractive. I've never wanted to see a dude's penis. I don't even want to look at my own.

The problem I faced back then is a problem I still encounter in my daily life as an adult. Stereotypes. Many people just don't expect a straight black male to enjoy cheesy boy band love songs or admit out loud that he cried watching Titanic. To this day there are still too many people who refuse to accept the fact that I'm straight.

My personality doesn't fit what is typically expected from an American black male. They can't deny my skin tone.

They could argue against my manhood but all I'd have to do is pull down my pants. So there's obviously only one good explanation left.

I briefly considered the possibility of a sex change. Obviously I never went through with it. There's nothing wrong with anyone who wants that for themselves but it wasn't for me. I never wanted to be a woman. I was just tired of being a man. I believed that if I was a butch lesbian people would stop questioning my personality and just accept me for who I am.

Also, sometimes I just get tired of my penis. This thing gets on my nerves. I'm getting close to thirty now and there are still times when I spend half the day spanking the monkey. Someone told me that my sex drive would diminish as I got older and my hormones calmed down. I'm still waiting for that to happen. There are some days when I just want to take a pair of scissors and hack it off. Not like I'm ever really going to need it.

In addition to my growth as a person I experienced an even more substantial growth as a writer. I wrote my first movie. For over a year I'd been writing song after song. One day I decided to put a bunch of them together and write a story around them. Later in the year I'd also begin writing my first ever TV show. The original title is incredibly stupid and potentially insensitive so we'll go by the current title…Amanda's Little Brother.

The show started because in those younger days I was still experimenting with my music. My basic style is mostly based in R&B/soul ballads. Especially the classic styles from Motown artist of the 80s and early 90s. That year Nickelback released their album All the Right Reasons. My friend Brett bought the album and I listened to it a few times. I loved every single song and decided I would try writing rock music.

I was pushing myself out of my comfort zone so I struggled at first. This new style I was trying out became the focus of my life for the next few months. As I was writing this new music I started wondering if there was any possibility that I could actually get an existing rock band that would want to perform these songs. That's why I came up with the idea to make Amanda's Little Brother. A TV show about a bunch of high school kids making a band together.

CHAPTER 14

Junior Year

The summer before my junior year I went to a Spurs basketball camp. I missed the first day. I got lost on the way there. The next morning my grandmother rode the bus with me to make sure I got off on the right spot.

My first day was brutal. These other teenagers were all in great shape and many of them had plans to actually play for the NBA. It was a good gift but it wasn't something I really wanted. They really pushed you. I was so far behind everyone else in my age group that they put me with the middle schoolers.

There were a couple of good things that happened. I couldn't dribble or score but I got a certificate for best rebounder. I also got a couple of blocks in every game we played. The most important part of the entire camp, the only reason I even agreed to go in the first place, was that I got to meet a few of the Spurs. I'd already met a couple of guys before. Avery Johnson once and David Robinson twice. Now I got to meet Bruce Bowen and get his autograph.

I also got to meet George "Iceman" Gervin. He made everyone split into teams of three and we'd compete against each other in a shooting tournament. First team to ten wins.

My team lost ten to five in the first game. I made zero of the five shots I attempted. Every time I missed a shot I hurried over to grab the ball and bounce it back to my teammates. When the game was over Iceman sought me out. He shook my hand and said he loved my hustle.

A lot of things were changing with band. Schroeder took over as section leader and Andre became assistant drum major. During the summer we had a sectional at the mall and ended up playing a game of hide and seek. No one told me that they were playing this game. We were all just sitting down eating lunch when they all got up to use the restroom at the same time. After a while I started getting suspicious and went to the restroom to see if they were all taking massive dumps. When I saw an empty restroom, I started wondering around the mall finding them one by one in random stores.

My junior year of high school can be summed up with a single name…Miranda. She was a flute player in the band. She was only two or three inches shorter than me. If she was any paler, she'd be see-through.

We were in the same grade but she was in science academy so we've never had a single class together. Before that summer I didn't even consider her a friend. She was just another person in the band. I'm not sure when that changed or why. One day she smiled at me and my heart fluttered.

Miranda is the reason I stopped believing in fairy tales. She was my Belle. Incredibly smart, beautiful and kind. It was ridiculous of me to ever believe someone like her could ever possibly fall in love with someone like me. I realize that now but as a teen I was stupidly hopeful that all the stories were true. That all those cheesy love songs I listened to might have actually meant something. I was wrong. It wouldn't be right to call Miranda the one that got away. They all got away. Instead I'll say that Miranda is the one I'll never get over.

The band getting another two at UIL. It didn't hurt as much this year. I expected it this time. For the second year in a row the football team made the playoffs. I went to the first game but not the second. I kept failing calculus. This was the year I stopped giving any effort in school. I started skipping classes.

My friends where all in fourth period lunch but I had fifth period. I kept skipping fourth period to hang out with them. Then in fifth period I'd just post up on a wall and write the whole time. The classes I did go to I'd either sleep the entire time or completely ignore the teacher and work on a song or one of my stories.

Before marching season ended Miranda started acting weird around me. One day I asked her if we were still friends and she said "I guess." I had to ask a friend what that meant. I was told that it either means "I'm not sure" or "no, but I don't want to hurt your feelings." Either way it definitely does not mean yes.

I stopped talking to her. I never stopped writing songs about her. I even started imagining what life would be like if we were married. Wondering what our children would look like. I never stopped dreaming about her.

With December approaching the band threw another Christmas party this year. The day of the party I went to the band hall as soon as school ended. I was just hanging around waiting for the fun to start when I happened to see a young girl just sitting on the floor with her back against the lockers.

I've spent most of my life feeling alone and afraid. Seeing her curled up against the wall like that made me want to help her. I ended up spending the entire night with her. For the longest time we just sat there talking. Once the party was getting started, I dragged her out to the dance floor with me. She was nervous because she didn't know how to dance. Neither did I. Sometimes you just have to cut loose and have a good time.

Some rumors started going around the band that I had a crush on her. I decided to let people think that. I never had any feelings for her. In fact the entire night as I talked with her and we danced our hearts away…I couldn't stop my head from turning in a different direction.

I spent that entire night fighting with every fiber of my being to not stare at Miranda. Wishing that I could hold her in my arms as the music played. I would've given anything just for the chance to be closer to her. I cried myself to sleep that night.

When the second semester came around, I found the courage to ask Miranda if it was ever possible that we could be friends again. She said she couldn't be friends with me if

I liked her. So I lied and said I was over her. The feelings were all still there. I just got much better at hiding them.

All through high school I never once participated in concert UIL. I always managed to fail at least one class. This year came as a bit of a shock. For the first time all year I had a passing grade in calculus. It was only 72 but passing is passing. The only hiccup was AP English.

I skipped school on a day when we had a test. I was given a zero and my grade in the class dropped to a 58. I took the test the very next day but the teacher never put the grade in the books. That 58 remains to this day. I had to ace the class for the rest of the year just to pass with a 70. In the next two grading periods I got a 93 and a 98 and barely passed for the year with a D.

The most impressive thing about those grades was the fact that I skipped so much school. There was a three-month period of time were if I went to school at all it would only be on a Friday because that's when teachers would usually give their tests. Still, when the TAKS test came around not only did I pass I got commended on three of the four subjects including a perfect score in history.

I was one correct answer short of getting commended in science. That was the hardest subject for every single person who took the test. The absences were piling up and the school was starting to crack down. That's actually the only reason I even showed up to take the TAKS test.

One spring afternoon I was playing basketball with Mike D and our group of friends. I jumped up to grab a rebound.

When I came down my foot slipped and my ankle bent much further than any ankle ever should. I fell to the ground and grabbed my ankle.

I was in excruciating pain but the guys were telling me to stop being a pussy and get up. They helped me onto my feet and I kept playing. When I went home everything felt normal. When I woke up the next morning, I took one step out of bed and instantly doubled over in pain. I stayed in bed all day.

The next morning my grandmother took me to see a doctor. I weighed in at 263 pounds. Well, that explains why none of my clothes fit anymore. The last time I was weighed was at the end of middle school. Over a three-year span I went from five feet six inches tall weighing 160 pounds to five feet ten inches tall and weighing 260 pounds.

My weight gain was the result of the horrible eating habits I developed. Food was my main source of comfort. There were also times when I'd get so depressed that I might go a day or two without eating anything at all. Overall my weight was constantly trending up.

The doctor took x-rays of my ankle. I was told I hard torn ligaments. It wasn't a major injury. I wouldn't require surgery. I had no loss of motion in my foot. It was just very painful. The doctor gave me a prescription for one month of painkillers. My mom would buy a brace for me to wear on my ankle. The painkillers worked very well. One pill and I could make it through an entire day without any pain in my ankle.

That was the problem. They worked too well. I found myself thinking, "If one pill can erase this much pain maybe taking all of them at once could completely erase my pain." I'd already been taking the pills for over a week. There were twenty left in the bottle. I chugged them all and went to sleep hoping I would never wake up again.

Earlier that year I had been to see a phycologist. I saw him once a week for about three months. That's where I first got diagnosed with depression. He determined that I might need medication to help with my condition. He kept trying to recommend me to a psychiatrist he knows.

In my final session with him I finally agreed. It wasn't because I wanted to get better. It was because I'd seen people on TV kill themselves by taking anti-depressants. As I was walking out the door, I changed my mind and left without making an appointment.

Everything Is Impossible

CHAPTER 15

Senior Year

My hair has always been a source of contention. From an early age every memory I have of my hair was felt with hatred. I have very thick and very curly hair. This combination makes it very hard to manage. I didn't care enough about how I looked to be bothered with brushing it every day. I don't think I've ever used Shampoo.

My grandmother would make sure to cut my hair every two weeks. She would also make sure to sit me down in front of her to brush it. I remember one specific time when she brushed my head so hard that it made me cry. She laughed. She probably thought that I hated when my hair looked good. Nope. I was crying because it felt like every single strand of hair had been yanked out of my scalp. I didn't care how I looked. My head was throbbing.

Once my grandmother moved out my hair never got brushed. By the time I got into high school she had retired her clippers. It had been growing for over two years and I'd barely touched it at all. I'd done a few things with it from time to time. One time last year I'd used a straightening iron to get the knots out of my hair and reveal the afro. As soon as the hair got wet it knotted right back up again.

I decided to try again. Halfway to school a bird pooped on my hair. I washed it out as soon as I got to school. That side of my hair shriveled up again. I decided to even it out by wetting the other side. When I realized my hair looked like Vegeta's I thought, "Awesome" and just left it like that for the rest of the day.

Since I'm talking about my hair should I mention my beard? I'm pretty sure it started growing sometime in high school. I couldn't tell you exactly when. At some point I did start shaving. Mostly because during marching season we were told we had to. I was never taught how to shave. I stole one of my mom's disposable razors and just tried to mimic the things I'd seen on TV. I cut myself a few times. They were all tiny cuts and they only happened every now and then.

The summer before my senior year my grandfather came to visit. He hated how my hair looked. He said I either had to do something with my nappy head or shave it off. He took me to a barber shop and we scheduled an appointment. A week later I had cornrows. At first I thought it was the coolest thing I've ever done. A week later I was already tired of them. They hurt my head and made it hot.

After nearly three months I got frustrated and yanked them all out. That's when a miracle happened. I looked in the mirror and realized I had Corbin Blue's hair style. I thought I was so cool. That excitement went away very quickly. It took too much effort to take care of. I'm talking two or three hours of brushing a day. After three days I got tired of it and shaved it all off. Corbin had that haircut for years. How did you do it bro?

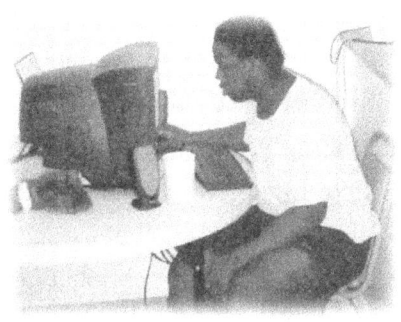

That year I started watching more anime. I had plenty of exposure to anime throughout my life but it was because of Joe's influence that I started actively seeking anime out. He started introducing me to subbed anime.

Joe had a taste for gory anime like Higurashi and School Days. I didn't like those as much. I did love some of the other shows he introduced me to. Things like Love Hina and Ouran High School Host Club. I kept branching out from there. Watching shows like School Rumble, Revolutionary Girl Utena and the dub of Gakkou No Kaidan.

Anime is the reason I first started watching YouTube. Before copyrights started becoming an issue, I found all my anime on that site. I was also able to find some of my favorite classic shows like Mighty Morphin' Power Rangers and Digimon. Senior year if I wasn't at school, I was most likely at home either playing video games, watching porn or watching shows on YouTube.

This year I began writing more seriously. I started considering the very real possibility of making it a career for myself. I started working on Oscar's storyline. I started scaling down his powers. I was watching an episode of The Simpsons and Bart was looking at a Radioactive Man comic book.

I decided Oscar's only power would be radiation. If I couldn't explain how radiation would give him a certain ability then I would remove that ability. I also had him start interacting with some of the other standalone heroes I had created. I merged them all together into one universe.

I realized too late that I might have been able to skip my senior year of high school. If I had passed all my classes junior year, I would've already had enough credits to graduate. There would've only been a couple of required classes that I could've tested out of during summer.

Instead, I have a senior year where I have no classes with my friends and half of them are the exact same classes I took last year. Good news: at our school seniors have permission to leave campus for lunch. Some days even when it wasn't my lunch period, I'd just walk out the door and go home for the day.

I also had eighth period free. If I didn't have practice after school I got to go home early. When we did have practice, I'd normally do one of two things. Sometimes I'd practice with the A1 band. Many times, I'd just sit in the bleachers next to our practice field either staring at the sky or watching grass grow.

The only class I enjoyed that year was creative writing. For the past two years I spent most of class time writing songs or working on stories. It was great to have a class where that's what I get graded for. One of the many projects I worked on that year was a new song called Memories.

I suddenly found myself having a resurgence of feelings for Jamie. I talked to Elise about it and she told me that I was only having those feelings because Jamie was the last girlfriend I had. Elise was having some of those feelings for her most recent ex-boyfriend.

That conversation inspired me to write the greatest masterpiece of my high school days. A song about how on the coldest nights the crushing weight of loneliness can make you forget all the negative things about the relationship and beg for the days when you had someone to hold in your arms.

> **Cause this feels less right**
> **As each day goes by**
> **I'm dying by myself**

Other than creative writing, band was the only reason I bothered showing up to school. We were busier than usual this year. It seemed like we had a different event every weekend. Every Friday a game, every Saturday some sort of parade or competition.

We only had four tuba players that year. One in each grade. I hated that freshman so much. He was confident. He took no shit. It was exasperating. I was so frightened when I came into high school. I was looking forward to some of that good-natured hazing. He fought back so we stopped trying. Anything short of physical violence wasn't going to break this guy. It wasn't worth it.

No matter how frustrating band could get it was the only thing that kept me going. This was my last chance to get a one at UIL. I wasn't planning on going to college and even if I did, I had no intention of continuing with band. After this year I'd never march again. I worked my ass off every single day. That led to me hurting my shoulder.

It wasn't a gruesome injury. Just a little strain. I went to see a doctor and got a prescription. One bottle of pain killers and one bottle of muscle relaxers. I went to the doctors because I was experiencing sincere pain. I wasn't planning to get pills. The moment those bottles were in my hand I knew exactly what I would do with them.

I opened those bottles once. I don't remember the exact calendar date. I believe it was in October. I know for sure it was a week before UIL because that was the only reason, I could think of to not kill myself. No one loved me. No one would miss me if I was gone. The only people who would even notice I was missing are my relatives. They'd only show up to the funeral out of some misguided sense of obligation. A few people might shed tears. Then a month later they will have completely forgotten I ever existed in the first place.

I could only think of one reason not to kill myself. UIL was next week. We only had four tuba players. If I die right now there's no possible way, they could make the necessary adjustments in time. They might have to drop out of UIL completely. That's why I decided to kill myself. The only reason I could come up with for why I needed to say alive was that the band wouldn't have enough people. I was just a body there to take up space. I wasn't important. No one needed me.

That Saturday night, with MadTV on my television screen, I emptied both bottles into my stomach. There were thirty pain killers and thirty muscle relaxers. I'm still not sure what pain killers are or how they work. There is one thing I know for sure: the heart is a muscle. The lungs are muscles. My hope was that enough of those pills in my system might completely shut down one or both of those. I grabbed a bottle of water. I took the pills one by one, taking a sip of water with each one. When the last pill was swallow, I laid back in bed and closed my eyes hoping I'd never open them again.

The next morning the sun poked through the blinds hitting me right in the eyes. That early in the morning I didn't stop to think about the fact that my suicide had failed. The only thought on my mind was "ouch. Too bright." I tried to roll over but my body wouldn't move.

I tried to lift my arms. They wouldn't respond. I tried to sit up. My neck was the only thing that moved. The rest of my body was paralyzed. At least we know the muscle relaxers worked. My tongue was paralyzed as well. It just hung there limp. I started worrying that I might choke on it.

The most painful part of this entire ordeal was the fact that no one ever knew what happened that day. My entire life I would've killed for just a little bit of privacy. I've lost count of how many times someone walked in on me when I was masturbating. Yet the one time I would've been thankful for the intrusion was the only day in my life when I was actually left alone.

No one came to check on me. Not one single knock. Not even shouting at me through the door to ask if I was awake or hungry. Not one person called the house looking for me. If I had died that day it's entirely possible that no one would've found out until Tuesday. That made me cry. They were proving me right. No one cares.

I lied there all day, trapped in my own body. I ate nothing. Drank nothing. I peed and pooped multiple times. My bowels were too relaxed. The poop just slid right out. I tried to scream but all that came out was garbled noise.

At least the day was a complete waste. I left my TV on. I was able to watch the Cowboys beat the Raiders. I got to see a new episode of The Simpsons. Best of all, I eventually fell asleep. I woke up the next morning and my body was working again. I threw away my soiled underwear, took a shower and went to school. I kept living my life as if that day never happened.

The day before UIL all the seniors in band took turns standing in front of the band and giving an inspirational speech. When my turn came, I decided to tell them the story of my experience in high school band. I told them that my freshman year we were so talented that I never really felt like I had to try. I told them how I got so nervous at UIL that I didn't play a single note. How we got a one but I felt no sense of accomplishment.

I told them how close I came to quitting. That I didn't think band was for me. Then I heard we were getting new band directors and decided to give them a chance. I told them how much harder I worked the next two years. How even though it was disappointing to get a two, I was more proud of those twos than I could ever be of that one.

I told them that I've been watching them since summer and I know how hard they've all worked. That no matter what score the judges gave them they should be proud of themselves. Them I performed a rap that I wrote just for the occasion.

As I walked back to my seat Foster stopped me and told me I was his hero. I didn't feel like a hero. I felt like a fraud. I didn't believe the words I was saying. What right did I have to say them after what I did? I'm like a life coach who's forced to go to rehab after snorting coke and crashing his car into a kindergarten classroom. What right do I have to tell these people anything?

The band performed well at UIL and we received a one. It was one of the proudest moments of my life. After that, I barely showed up for school at all. I wasn't doing any work. At this rate I was in very real danger of having a fifth year of high school. Then my mother found a school called the Excel Academy. It was an organization built to prevent at risk students from becoming dropouts.

When we first showed up, they looked at my transcripts and said that I didn't qualify. My only risk was a lack of effort. They weren't going to accept me. Then my mother started crying and they changed their mind. That's a great trick. I wish I could do that.

Once I was accepted, I transferred immediately. I personally believe there should be more schools that operate like Excel Academy did. Let people learn at their own rate. The biggest problem I had with high school is that it lasted three years longer than it needed to. I got bored because I felt like I wasn't learning anything. I stopped trying.

I was able to be successful at Excel Academy because I actually got back what I put in. It took me one month to get my diploma. It wasn't the material that made school suck. It was how that material got presented. Doing things my way in my own time suddenly made learning fun again.

Not only was school more fun but so was writing. I didn't have the stress of being forced to sit through eight mind numbing hours of useless lectures and studying. I wasn't forced to trudge through crowded halls. The added sense of comfort helped my creativity flow so much more freely. I did some of my best writing during that time frame. There was one show I started working on that marked a new period of growth in my storytelling.

It started when I was studying English. I read a Robert Frost Poem titled Fire & Ice and didn't understand one word of it. I asked the teacher the meaning and he said that if you put a block of ice above a fire then that fire will melt the block of ice. As the block of ice is melting the water will douse the fire. In the end, all you're left with is a pile of wet ashes. I read the poem again and have no idea where that explanation came from. Well, since he's the one grading the papers, I went off what he said.

His explanation gave me an idea for a tragic romance. The story of two opposing forces destined to destroy each other.

I titled it Fire & Ice in honor of the poem that inspired it. I wanted to try something different for this story. I tried swapping gender roles. Gave the man a personality that was stereotypically female and the woman a personality that was stereotypically male. My misguided attempt to change the status quo resulted in me writing the same basic average love story you always see. That concept still exists in a different story but for Fire & Ice I chose to go in a different direction.

At that time there were two incredibly popular TV shows called The L Word and South of Nowhere that had main characters who were gay women. It gave me the idea to turn the male lead in Fire and Ice into a female. It was the first LGBT storyline I ever wrote. Once I made that one simple change to the character the story began to write itself. I took a brief pause to look at what I was creating and wondered if I should throw it away. What right do I, a straight man, have to write about gay women?

I thought of 7th Heaven. The show ran for eleven seasons, airing over two hundred episodes. When I stopped to think about the long history of the show there was something I noticed. I couldn't remember a single mention of homosexuality or abortion. It makes sense. The show is religion based. You can't take a hard stance on either of those issues without alienating half your audience. If you don't take a hard stance one way or the other you run the risk of potentially pissing off your entire audience.

Something occurred to me in that moment. In my fantasy life I exclude celebrities I don't like. I ignore movies, TV shows and romances that don't fit the narrative I want. If I went out of my way to never write a single gay character in any of my stories it'll basically feel the same as me saying that I don't think they should exist. So I moved forward with Fire & ice.

It was the first LGBT storyline I ever wrote. It's the first story I've ever written where the main character wasn't based off myself. It's the first show I've written that didn't star teenagers. As I was writing the story, I realized that it would probably take at least ten years before the story ever got made. With that in mind I wrote the lead characters in their late twenties to early thirties so Gabrielle Christian and Mandy Musgrave could play them.

You might have noticed that I've spent the previous paragraphs ignoring reality for the sake of stories I was writing. I wrote the paragraphs like that because that's how I was living my life at the time. I wasn't thinking about my future. I never took the SAT. I never applied to a single college. I never tried to find a job and had no plans to do any of the above things.

I only had one plan in mind for the future. I talked to my uncle and asked if I could move in with him. I finished all my classes at Excel the first week of January. As soon I finished the last class, I packed my clothes and spiral notebooks into a suitcase. I packed all my DVDs into a big box that my mom would mail to me later. In the middle of January, I got on a plane and flew to Wisconsin.

CHAPTER 16

Wisconsin

January in Wisconsin is unbearably cold. I got off the plane and my uncle was waiting for me. I've gotten bigger since I last saw him but he's still a few inches taller than me. He's getting closer to fifty but doesn't have many wrinkles yet. His hair line is thin and receding. He had a protruding belly, though not quite as large as mine.

When he took me back to the duplex that he shares with his roommate the first thing my uncle did was make me take a shower. They used bar soap. I hate bar soap. Especially when I'm expected to share it with other people. You're actually expecting me to clean my face with the same thing you use to clean your ass, feet and balls? I would always steal a bar for myself and keep it hidden in my room.

My early days in Wisconsin were even more frustrating than it was at home. It was a two-bedroom apartment. My uncle slept in the basement and used one of the bedrooms as storage space. They gave me that bedroom. He would burst into that room four times an hour. I was living there for more than three months before I could masturbate without worrying that he was going to burst through the door unannounced.

On top of that, I had nothing of my own in that place. I could only watch TV if no one else was. I could only use the computer if someone else wasn't on it. I could only use the PlayStation if someone else wasn't using the PlayStation or watching TV.

They had a Tuesday tradition of inviting friends from work to watch movies. When I first got there, I was happy to join them. It would later become a point of contention. My uncle always told me that it was my choice if I wanted to participate or not. Any time I didn't want to attend he would try to make me feel guilty. If I did show up there were dress codes and behavioral standards. Not to mention all the times when they picked horrible movies that I just didn't want to see. It reached a point where I refused to participate.

Looking at my uncle through a fresh pair of eyes I began to notice flaws. The things that bothered me most were the fact that he's incredibly condescending and hypocritical. He's got hard and fast rules for how people are supposed to live their lives. Then he'll break those rules every time the opportunity pops up. Like with cooking.

He's chastised me at times just for adding salt. Then he'll force me to cook, which I hate doing anyway, and without taking a single bite start adding a pinch of this and a sprinkle of that.

I remember hating the majority of meals that he made for one reason or another. There was one time when he made a bunch of barbeque cocktail wienies. I told him that I hated barbeque sauce. He said he would either put some to the side for me or that he wouldn't put the sauce on too heavy. He did neither of those things.

Every single sausage was drenched in barbeque sauce. So I took some in a bowl and washed them in the sink. By washed I mean I thoroughly rinsed them with water over and over again. Then threw them in the microwave for a minute.

Another time he was making meatloaf when I saw him chopping onions. I told him I didn't like onions. He said he'd chop them up so small that I wouldn't even notice them. I didn't swallow a single onion that day.

I spent about twenty minutes going through the meat with a fork picking out every onion I saw. There were some really tiny ones that I couldn't see with my eyes. I was able to feel them out with my tongue and teeth. I kept spitting tiny onion bits onto the plate.

I love video games. I play them because they're fun. One of my favorite games was Madden. My uncle says that the one thing he hates about the game is that it's skill of the player and not skill of the character. He hates that people go on about "I'm LT. Look at all the touchdowns I'm scoring." He preferred to just do coach mode.

Then there would be times when my uncle would try to hit on girls by telling them he played bass. That he was in a band. The only time he's ever played guitar is when he plays rock band in the living room. Yet he gets mad at me for playing Madden the wrong way. I like being able to say that I'm LT but I'd never actually try out for a football team. Much less lie and say I was on one.

I was feeling much more comfortable by the time I began my second year in Wisconsin. I now had a TV and PlayStation of my very own. They were both hand me downs but now I only have to leave my bedroom to use the computer. Also, I had my very own computer now so I could use it any time I please.

I wrote more songs, movies and TV shows on that year than any other point in my life. I finally gave Oscar a superhero name. I was listening to music while I was typing when a Britney Spears song started playing. When I heard that music, I started imagining a cartoon opening in my head. In that moment it just felt right that Oscar's superhero name should be Toxic.

Somewhere in that time period my uncle's best friend Scott moved in. I've known this guy since I was born and have always thought of him as a second uncle. He was the one who got me my first job.

When I first arrived, my uncle was ok with me just lazing about the house as long as I helped with chores. I would do things like shoveling snow out of the driveway, or cooking and cleaning from time to time. As time kept passing, he began losing patience. It didn't matter if I got a job or went to school, he just wanted me to do something with my life.

Scott got me a job as a dishwasher at the restaurant where he cooked. It wasn't a glamorous job but it also wasn't difficult. I worked Friday, Saturday and Sunday nights. All the other dishwashers there were high school boys. Once I got the job, I got my first bank account. Since I had income now my uncle made me pay one hundred dollars a month for rent. I also started sneaking out of the house to go buy my own snack food that I kept hidden in the closet.

I had built a decent living for myself. I hated every second of it. I never stopped wanting more. I never stopped watching celebrity interviews and wishing I was there. I never stopped listening to the radio wishing I could hear one of my songs.

I had spent the past three years wondering what I wanted to do with my life. What do I want to be when I grow up? I still wasn't sure how to answer that question. Then I remembered something that Whoopi Goldberg said in Sister Act 2. I haven't seen the movie in years so I don't remember the exact words. It was something along the lines of, "If you wake up in the morning and want to sing then you're a singer."

That didn't answer all my questions but there was one thing I knew for sure… I liked writing songs. I liked creating these stories. I liked building these worlds. For the first time in my life I actually had a goal. I want to spend the rest of my life creating these stories and sharing them with the world.

That's who I am. I even wrote a song about it. I titled it Necessity. I wrote it to serve as a constant reminder of what I was working toward and why I was working so hard. I didn't know back then how many times I would need that reminder.

It's more than a dream to me,
more than a fantasy
It's what my future holds, all that I ever see
It's more than a dream to me,
more than a fantasy
It's not something I want, it's a necessity

CHAPTER 17

Road to Haven

I planned it very carefully. I spent two months saving up money. I bought a plane ticket and planned my departure for that little window of space where my uncle has left for work, his roommate hasn't come back yet and Scott is still asleep. I called and scheduled a cab to arrive at one in the afternoon to take me to the airport.

Before I left, I ate all the ice cream in the fridge. I packed my favorite shirts, DVDs, books and a few other assorted items into one suitcase and a bowling bag. The only pair of pants I had were the ones I was wearing. Before I walked out the door, I left notes everywhere saying "Sometimes goodbye is a second chance."

The taxi took me to the airport where I got on this rickety little plane. It took us to the nearest city where we got on real airplanes to take us to our destinations. As I was looking out the window, I thought about Party in the U.S.A. I figured it wouldn't happen exactly like that but I was still excited about the possibilities that lie ahead. Turns out that song only applies to people who already have jobs and money. When my plane landed at the Los Angeles international airport, I found nothing but confusion. I was wondering around for about an hour not sure where to go or what to do.

I ended up getting frustrated and just stopped. I sat on my suitcase in front of what I discovered was a police station. The cops thought I was suspicious and came over to question me. Even though he was frisking me and asking all kinds of questions he was still being very kind. He just wanted to know what the situation was.

I definitely left out a few details. When he asked me if I was a runaway I lied to his face. I understand he has to ask that question but it's kind of stupid. The majority of runaways would not admit it to a cop.

He told me how to get into the city. You take this bus to here then this bus to there. Most of the bus drivers were pretty nice. There was one grumpy old black guy who didn't want to give me the time of day.

Before I knew it, I found myself stranded at a bus stop waiting for a bus that never came. A homeless couple showed up. They had it planned out. Brought their blanket and everything. I somehow managed to fall asleep. I was woken up around two o'clock by a freezing cold rain.

The next day the friendly bus drivers returned and they helped me find the way to Hollywood Boulevard where I spent the day just walking around. I stopped to look at every single star. I took note of all the stores. I located a couple of hostels.

At the end of the day I found myself getting on a bus and heading back. I ended up spending the night at a transfer station. I didn't sleep that night either. I went thirty-six hours with no food, nothing to drink, no peeing or pooping and two hours of sleep.

The next day I got on a bus back to Hollywood and checked out the hostels. The first one I went to was specifically for foreign travelers. In order to stay there, you needed to bring some sort of proof that you came from some other country. They told me there was another hostel just down the street.

If I remember correctly a room with four beds cost twenty-five dollars a day while a room with six beds cost twenty dollars a day. I decided to take the room with less risk of strangers. I regret that. They chose to put me in the worst possible room. I only had one roommate. His snoring is still the worst I have ever heard in my life.

When I first got to the room, I took a quick shower then jumped right into bed. Two days without sleep was plenty. I was excited to be in a bed again. Halfway through the night I was woken by the worst noise I've ever heard. Have you ever been hungover? Or had a migraine? Imagine you're dealing with both of those things… then someone turns on a jackhammer two centimeters from your face.

It was like that the entire time I stayed there. If he was in the room I was not. I just couldn't sleep through that snoring. My sleep schedule revolved entirely around his. Some nights I'd watch TV till the sun came out then spend all day asleep in bed.

The main thing I learned there is that good things don't just magically happen. I knew it was a longshot but a small part of me was hoping that maybe I'd just bump into a celebrity and impress them with my talent. They'd introduce me to all their friends and suddenly I have a career. It didn't work out that way. Those opportunities only presented themselves a couple of times.

Once as I was walking down the boulevard a couple of young black guys excitedly hurried to me and said that Sean Kingston was shopping in a nearby clothing store. As I walked by the store I looked in and saw him.

I thought about just walking up to him, introducing myself and singing some of the songs I'd written. I'd impress him with my lyrical genius and he'd take me straight to the studio to start laying down tracks. I decided against this for multiple reasons. Partly fear, partly out of consideration for him and partly because I was never a big fan of his music.

I stopped by to see a couple of tapings of Jimmy Kimmel Live. The first time was just to see how it all works. Before the show they asked if any of the audience members wanted to get on stage and show off their talents. That would be my way in.

I went back on a different day. When the talent portion arrived, I volunteered. The warm up comedian made fun of me three times before I even made it down the steps.

I got onstage and sang the chorus of my song Memories. The band played along. The audience seemed into it. After it was done, I said, "My name's gonna be on that walk of fame someday if you wanna help me out." The warm up guy said they couldn't help me out. Then he gave me a t-shirt and he sent me back to my seat. As I walked back a few people high fived me and told me how great I was. It felt good having strangers applaud my talent.

Living in LA proved to be quite expensive. I emptied my bank account before I left Wisconsin and ran out of money in a week. I had to keep begging my grandmother to send me money. I tried looking for work with zero success and the Hostel had a rule about not staying more than twenty-eight consecutive days. Most people who lived there would find someplace else to stay for a day, like a hotel or a friend's place, then come right back the day after.

I looked into multiple options before making my decision. This wasn't working. I needed a permanent place and this wasn't it. I decided to go home. My grandmother paid for a bus ticket. After twenty-eight days in LA I packed my bags and went back to San Antonio.

The bus ride wasn't the worst experience I've ever had but it came fairly close. The seats were a bit uncomfortable and I was surrounded by strangers. In the twenty-six hours that it took to get back to San Antonio I only got two hours of sleep. At least I wrote a great song.

I always wanted to write a song with the words far away in the title. Some of my favorite songs, from various artist like Staind, Nickelback and Rod Stewart, have had those words in the title. I wanted to make a song like Here Without

You or Right Here Waiting. I wrote the words Far Away at the top of the page and started thinking.

I was struggling at first. I couldn't find the inspiration. Not until I started thinking of Miranda. I hadn't seen her in two years. I hadn't talked to her in three years. Yet here I am still wanting to write songs about her.

I decided I wanted this to be the last love song I ever wrote for her. One song to get out all the feelings I still held inside. I added the word from to the beginning of the title. From Far Away. I knew I could never say it any better than this.

To this day I still consider it to be the best song I've ever written. A song about wanting to be closer to the person you love. A song about not being able to hold them in your arms. It was supposed to be a song about physical distance. Instead it was about emotional distance. Being in the same room as someone and feeling like you might as well be on the other side of the planet.

As the bus was passing through New Mexico we had some issues. For no reason at all the cops stopped the bus and boarded it demanding that every single person on board show them their ID. We all did exactly as they said. I was singled out.

I showed them my ID. I was compliant. They made me step off the bus. They searched my bag, frisked me and asked me all kinds of questions. I was eventually cleared of all suspicion and allowed back on the bus. I was told that I looked suspicious because I seemed reluctant to talk to them. I'm sleep deprived and have been stuck in this uncomfortable seat for hours when you suddenly storm the bus for no reason. Why would I want to talk to you?

When the bus arrived in San Antonio my mother was at the station waiting for me. I followed her back to her one-bedroom apartment. The life I lived there closely mirrored the life I lived in Wisconsin. I spent the majority of my time watching TV and looking at videos online.

I wrote some new songs and continued working on my stories. Meanwhile, my mother was struggling to find a job. She was falling behind on rent. We ate most of our meals at my grandmother's place. When she didn't have food to spare, we survived on a diet of plain white rice.

My mother and I were not getting along. We even had a fist fight. You might be feeling disgusted with me after reading that sentence. You might be appalled by the fact that a grown man would actually punch his mother. I have only one rule when it comes to fighting. I never throw the first punch. Other than that, all bets are off.

I don't care who you are. If someone is repeatedly punching me in the face, they better be ready to get punched right back. She wasn't ready. She punched me five times. All it took was one hit to make her stop.

Despite our turbulent relationship I have to give my mother credit. She was actively looking for a job. She was pounding the pavement for any way to pay the rent. Meanwhile, I spent my days relaxing in bed waiting for a miracle. I now realize how naïve I used to be when I was young.

I had an easy life. There was always food in the fridge. Always a roof over my head. Things generally had a way of working out for me. That's one thing that scared me about the future. Someone's always been there to take care of the difficult things. I was about to learn that sometimes life has a way of forcing you to grow up.

One morning my mom told me not to leave the apartment. Someone would come knock on the door. Don't let them in. In the middle of the day a man showed up and knocked on the door. I sat quietly and waited for him to leave.

After a few knocks he pulled out a key and unlocked the door. The deadbolt was still locked so the door wouldn't open. He broke the key in the lock then taped a bunch of papers to the door notifying us of our eviction. We spent the night packing as much of our stuff as we could.

We woke up at the crack of dawn so we could sneak out before management showed up. My mother called a cab to take us to my grandmother's place. We left all of our belongings with my grandmother then got on a bus headed downtown.

We arrived at the Haven for Hope intake office before the doors even opened. We signed our names on a sheet of paper then waited in the front for a few hours before a man took us to his office. He told us that we were being put on a list and we should come back next week.

For the next seven days my mother and I lived with my grandmother. I spent a week living in a one room apartment with two old women and no cable or video games. It was more than any teenage boy could ever bear.

Still, I appreciate what my grandmother did for us. She was staying at a senior living facility and received some warnings about us staying there. They have a rule about guest only staying for a few days at a time. She told them there was no way she'd let her family sleep on the streets.

The week passed and my mother and I made our way back to Haven, each with a suitcase full of clothes. Once again, we arrived before the doors opened. We wrote our names at the very top of a sheet of paper and waited for what felt like half a day before an old man called us back to his office. There was some confusion. We waited for hours to be told that we were being put on a waiting list. My mother made a fuss, including shedding a few tears. What a great trick. It works every time.

The man left the room for a few minutes. When he came back in, he told us to follow him to another room. We had our pictures taken and were given ID badges. Then we were escorted past security and onto the campus.

The men's dorm and women's dorm were on opposite sides of the campus. This was truly the beginning of a new chapter. For the first time in my life I wasn't sponging off one of my relatives. Instead I'm bunking with 800 total strangers. I kept a diary the entire time I was living at Haven. Maybe I'll publish it as my next book. As I write this, I refuse to look at it. I want this book to be entirely from memory.

Everything Is Impossible

CHAPTER 18

Haven for Hope – Part 1

The first two days that I lived at Haven I didn't step a single foot outside. I only left my bed to pee and shower. Then I met Kay. A tall fat black guy who only ever speaks by shouting at the top of his lungs. I don't know why he decided to talk to me but I'm glad he did. I would never have survived my time at Haven without him.

He showed me where the laundry room was, where to get soap, and most importantly where the cafeteria was. The food was never that great but when you're starving everything taste amazing. Kay also showed me how to get vouchers so I could go to the warehouse and get new clothes.

I was at Haven for a week when I found a note on my bed. I was summoned to the Transformational Center, generally referred to as the TC building, to meet my case manager Ron. He was responsible for making sure I successfully got back on my feet.

There were basic requirements for every new member of Haven. I had to take a test to measure my education level. I got a perfect score. They also had an anger management course. It was faith based so I ignored the majority of things the guy said.

During my introduction interview with Ron I mentioned my history with depression and suicides. He recommended I do community-based counseling. I had a therapist named Yolanda that I saw for over a year. Six weeks after meeting Ron I completed all my basics and was told I could move up to the second floor.

The dorm monitors were shocked when they were informed that I was moving. One of them said the words "but you've only been here two months." I was told at intake that it would only be one month before I moved up to the second floor. Apparently, it takes most people half a year.

The beds on the second floor were much bigger which meant less people to deal with. The lockers were also bigger so I brought my mom's desktop PC. I had no internet access but I could still sit there for hours on end working on my songs and stories.

The showers on the second floor were much better. They were still horrible. You push a button on a wall and a small stream of water comes out of the wall for a few seconds. At least with the upstairs bathrooms the stream was stronger, lasted longer and sometimes even got hot.

The longer I stayed at Haven the more people I met. It started with George and Abby. I saw them sitting together in the cafeteria and decided to say hi. It was a calculated move. In my brief time on campus I'd been watching the people around me and taking mental notes. I've seen these two talk to every single person on campus. So, either they know everybody on campus or they're just very friendly.

I decided to take a risk and say hi. It ended up being a great decision. George became one of the best friends I had at Haven.

Early on I got in the habit of going to my grandmother's place every Saturday. I'd clean some things around her apartment and she'd pay me with food. It took an hour to get there by bus. At some point in time I decided to walk. I'd wake up before the sun rose and make the three-hour walk in order to save myself one dollar and twenty cents. Not having any money at all really helped me learn the value of a dollar.

Every cent I had went to buying food. The food at Haven wasn't disgusting but it was never the best thing I'd ever eaten. Even when it tasted great there was never enough of it. I went down to 180 pounds. Some of you might think that's a high number but I was skin and bones. My body is naturally heavy. That was the only time in my adult life that I've ever been under 200 pounds. I was malnourished and incredibly lethargic.

After a few months at Haven a met a woman named Jennifer. She was a few years older than me and a few inches taller. She had long black hair and bronze skin. She always wore these giant hoop earrings. I hadn't asked a girl out since high school. I was never great at doing it in the first place but now I'm out of practice. It also didn't help that neither of us had said a single word to each other.

The only reason I was able to work up the courage to ask her out was because I knew she would say no. She was totally out of my league. I figured asking her out was just a good way to shake off the nerves and practice my technique.

When I expressed my interest in her Jen responded by informing me that she had five kids. I wanted to walk away. The little voice inside my head wouldn't let me. It kept telling me to try again. She hasn't said no yet. So I asked one more time. She told me that her last couple of relationships hadn't gone well and she wasn't in the mood for dating. She wouldn't date me but we could start as friends and see where it goes.

That night I ate dinner I with Jen and her children. She had five daughters. Destiny was eleven, Michelle was ten, Desiree was eight, Sandra was six and April was four. I was twenty and absolutely horrified. There were five little girls all staring at me with these big brown eyes. I was convinced that they knew exactly why I was here and the hated me for it. I hardly opened my mouth at all that night.

Jen was in my life for three months. After that she would pop up occasionally from time to time. I'm technically still in contact with her. Not like I was back then. Back then we spent time together every single day. I don't think I ever had sincere feelings for her. She was hot. I was horny. That was enough. I was young, lonely and stupid.

She led me to believe I actually stood a chance. I asked her directly on multiple occasions if she would consider dating me. One of those times she told me that she wasn't ready to date yet but the moment she was I'd be her first choice. I think she was hoping that if she waited long enough, I'd just get over her.

When we first met, I didn't pay much attention to Jen's daughters. After almost a month together they took over my entire life. I spent more time with them than I did with Jen. I would play with the kids while Jen was sitting on a bench gossiping with friends.

One night Desire asked me to tie her shoes. I remembered how hard it was for me to learn to tie my shoes when I was a kid. So when I bent down to tie her shoes I explained it every step I was doing. As I was finishing, she said to me, "I wish you were my daddy."

When those words hit my ears, my heart skipped a beat. Something inside me changed that day. I don't know how to explain it. It's a feeling you can only understand if you've already felt it. There was a fundamental shift in the very core of my being. I looked up and saw her smiling down at me with those big eyes. It took every ounce of strength in my body not to cry.

I told her to run along and play with her friends. As I stood there watching them play my heart grew heavy. It felt good to hear her say those words. I felt a type of happiness I never could've imagined. Then my heart sank like a block of concrete. Although I didn't want to admit it, I knew that these days wouldn't last.

I was trying my best to ignore some very obvious signs that the end was near. The most unmistakable sign was the fact that I overhead Jen talking with her friends about some really cute Puerto Rican named Mike. I spent a week trying to have a discussion with her. Am I always going to be just a friend or is there a real possibility of something happening here?

I should've realized back then that her refusal to give me a straight answer was in itself an answer. The day finally came when she asked Mike to be her boyfriend. He immediately sent one of his friends to warn me to stay away from his girl.

Jen told me I should back off for a while so I stopped all contact. It broke my heart. It wasn't about getting rejected this time. I was in pain because I couldn't see my kids. Knowing that I might never see them again felt like having my heart ripped right out of my chest. I didn't eat dinner that night. I went straight to bed and buried my head in the pillow.

Kay came over to talk to me. He told me that she wasn't worth being sad over. None of the girls in that place were good enough for me anyway. His words didn't help at all. The most painful thing about this all was the overwhelming doubt in my mind. That voice in my head telling me I'd spend the rest of my life lonely and miserable. I'll spend the rest of my life never feeling like anyone actually loves me.

That's why his presence did help a little bit. It felt good to know that he cared enough to come over and check on me. He couldn't stop me from being sad but I'm grateful that he was willing to try. That night I cried so much that my nose bled. Around three in the morning I still couldn't sleep. So I pulled out a pen and a spiral notebook. I wrote a song called My Daughters to say goodbye to Jen's girls.

CHAPTER 19

Haven for Hope – Part 2

When I first arrived at Haven I was told that a person is only allowed to stay there for a maximum of two years. I was fairly eager to get a job as quickly as possible so I could save money and leave this place.

They had a job placement program but it was useless. The woman I spoke to said they could only help you find jobs based on what you've got on your resume. Since the only job I had on my resume was dishwasher those were the only jobs she was allowed to point me towards. I never went back after that first visit.

There was also an education department that tried to get me into community college. Since I just got back from Wisconsin a few months ago I was considered an out of state student. The amount of money they charged me as more than what I'd get from the Pell grant. So school would not be an option until I'd been in San Antonio for at least a year to re-establish myself as a Texas resident. If I'd known that would happen, I would've lied on the application.

Haven also had some OJT (on the job training) programs that they would force people into. I was placed with custodial staff. I would spend a few hours a day at the intake office cleaning toilets, mopping floors and emptying trash cans. A few months into my stay at Haven a computer lab opened. Many people, including myself, would stay in there for hours on end.

That's why Member Connect was created. That way the computer lab could be monitored and people's usage could be regulated. Rather than hiring new people, or pulling current employees away from their duties, someone had the idea to let Haven residents run the computer lab. It would count as their OJT. I decided to join so I could stay on the computer all day. Most importantly, it meant I wouldn't have to clean toilets anymore.

Soon after that a new complication came into my life. Her name was Sandy. There's only one thing you need to know about Sandy… she is a succubus. This girl oozed pheromones from every pore in her body. I would like to say that everybody who met her wanted her but that isn't accurate. I didn't want her. I needed her. I couldn't be in the same room as her without wanting to caress every inch of her body with my tongue. Any time she walked past me I couldn't help but breathe her in. I wasn't in love. I was intoxicated.

I asked her out. As usual, I was turned down. She said she wasn't ready for dating but we could start as friends. Sound familiar? She said the exact same things that Jennifer did. The ending was fairly similar as well. I spent months of my life constantly yearning for her affection only to watch her find the arms of another. I felt a surge of emotions, strongest of which was anger. How did this happen twice in the same year? Worst of all, the guy she started dating was George.

Their relationship with each other strained the friendship between George and me. There were three separate occasions where one of us refused to talk to the other. Even when we were getting along well things were always a bit off. Mostly because any time we all hung out together the two of them couldn't keep their hands off each other.

They would sit there shoving their tongues down each other's throats. My only options were to either stand there trying not to stare and pretending that I don't want to take a sharp knife and shove it into George's crotch or leave. I chose the latter.

I started distancing myself from them. Member Connect became my main focus. I would volunteer for morning, afternoon and night shifts in order to get as much computer time as I could. I couldn't have predicted how much that decision would impact my life.

Other than George and Kay the most important people from my Haven days are the ones I met through Member Connect. One of those people was Michael Powers. He and I got off to a bit of a rocky start. The more time we spent together the more comfortable we became.

When I met Powers, I believe he was in his seventies. He was dealing with health issues so from time to time I'd go months on end without seeing him because he was stuck in a hospital. When he was around, he made me feel like a child. I've spent the majority of my life feeling like I was surrounded by idiots. Powers is one of the few people on this planet to ever make me feel stupid. I greatly enjoyed being able to pick his brain.

He helped me figure out so many things about myself. I remember one time we had a conversation where he quoted someone. I can't remember the guy's name. Apparently, this man once said "I realized my imaginary friends were imaginary because as I grew up, they didn't." I looked at Powers, legitimately puzzled, and I asked him, "Your imaginary friends aren't supposed to grow up with you?" He looked at me and said something along the lines of, "You might actually be crazy."

Even though they were said jokingly those words struck me. When I was six, I created an imaginary best friend named Lionel Evans. We used to look identical. As we aged, I started noticing subtle differences between us. He grew taller than me. His skin was lighter than mine. As I was getting fatter, he stayed in great shape. He also grew his hair until it got long enough for him to get dreadlocks.

In Middle school we had every single class together. Every year of high school we saw each other less and less. He was in science academy and left band after freshman year to focus on athletics. Halfway through our junior year he got a recording contract and moved to LA where he now lives with his wife and their daughter. I still talk to him from time to time. Every few years he'll stop by to ask me how I'm doing. I'll always say I'm doing better than I actually am so that he doesn't worry about me. He never believes my lies.

I can see my imaginary friends as easily as I can see anyone else. I can hear their voices as if they were really sitting beside me. It's not just in my head. They are real people to me. They'll say things that I never would think of.

There are only two things separating my imaginary friends from real people. Number one is that they never piss me off. The few times that my imaginary friends disagree with me I'll usually end up changing my mind to agree with them by the time the conversation is over. With normal humans it's much easier to dig in my heels and stubbornly stick to my ideals.

Number two is even more important. I can't touch my imaginary friends. When I hug Lionel or pet my animals all I feel is air. When I hug a human, I can feel the warmth of their body. That's why when I really like someone, I often find myself going out of my way to touch them.

Physical contact is how I verify that you are real. If I truly hate someone, I will go out of my way to never make any physical contact at all. That's my way of telling you "I hate you so much that I refuse to acknowledge your existence."

Meanwhile, in the middle of this self-evaluation, I met Mrs. Ruth Ann Ramon. Age: Unknown. Birthplace: Unknown. Favorite Color: Unknown. As many years as I've known this woman, I know very few things about her. All I can tell you is that she's got a kind heart and she loves Jesus.

Also, she's got four kids. Well, I like to think of myself as her adopted child but there are only four that's she's actually given birth to. One of them is the same age as me.

I've never met her. I've been told stories and shown pictures but I've never been in the same room as her. I don't know if I've ever been in the same city as her. Mostly just mentioning her because it felt rude not to.

I'll focus on the three kids I did meet. Their names were Maryssa, Jacinda and Jedi. If I remember correctly at the time, Jedi was twelve, Jacinda was sixteen and Maryssa was seventeen. If I'm not remembering correctly, they'll be sure to tell me. The first thing I remember about Maryssa is that she always seemed angry. It's possible that she just has the worst case of resting bitch face ever. Jedi and Jacinda feared her. I am not now nor have I ever been afraid of Maryssa. I do however strongly refrain from angering her out of respect for the fact that she probably could kill me with her bare hands.

I like Maryssa. She's a fantastic person. That being said, I had a much easier time connecting with the other two. I have no hesitation in saying that Jedi and Jacinda really do feel like my little brother and sister. Jedi is a special kid. I don't think I can ever say enough good things about this guy. If he ran for president, I'd vote for him. Even though he's not even twenty yet.

Jacinda... well... she reminds me of myself for all the worst reasons. Smart enough to take over the world but completely lacking direction. Like Jedi and Maryssa, I know I don't really have to worry about Jacinda. I can tell that's no matter what she'll find her way through life. I just don't want her to struggle as much as I did.

I worked hard to distance myself from people at Haven. I didn't want to be part of that world. Problem is, I kept meeting people like the Kay, George, Powers, the Ramones and many others that aren't mentioned in this book.

There was a lot of drama that happened in that place. There was a girl named Amy who lied about being pregnant. Despite the mounting evidence that she was lying I continued to take her side. Why? Because Jen let Amy babysit her girls. I spent months of my life pretending to believe her lie because it meant that every now and then I'd get to see my daughters.

There was a young man named Matthew. I was told he suffered from Asperger's syndrome. I don't know how we got paired together in the first place but somehow, we became good friends. I felt more like a babysitter. I don't know why everyone expected me to be his handler.

I liked the guy. I really did. He's a good kid with a kind heart. I sincerely enjoyed spending time with him. It just got so frustrating after a while. It felt like I was constantly trying to wrangle a giant four-year-old. He would move away after a while. I was sad to see him go but also a bit relieved. His situation was too much for me to handle.

There was one final romantic interest at Haven. Her name was Maya. I don't remember how I met her. She had been there for a while before we started talking. She was about my age, maybe a year younger. Very Skinny, very pale, thin hair. Honestly looked kind of sickly.

Thinking back, I can't remember what it was about her that first got my attention. Something about being around her just felt right. Unfortunately, history repeats itself. She already had someone she liked. The only reason they weren't dating is because the situation was complicated.

While I have many fond memories of her, I almost left her out of this book entirely. The reason I decided to write about her is because of something she taught. In our time together, and our time apart, I noticed something about her. She kept the letters I gave her. She held on to the songs I wrote for her. She carried them around in her pockets. Sandy had done the same thing.

It made me realize something. I was told that girls love when a guy writes songs for her. It's true. Even if she doesn't like the guy, she'll appreciate the song. It won't make her love you. I spent over seven years of my life writing music daily. I went from writing two or three songs a day to two or three songs a year.

Meanwhile, I kept moving up the ranks in Member Connect. By simply being there long enough I kept getting promoted. People kept leaving and the best person left gets promoted to fill the vacant spot.

As the months passed, I went from a simple lab proctor all the way to Program Manager. Basically, I was responsible for every single thing that happened with Member Connect. The only people allowed to tell me what to do were Haven staff members.

At one point in time Haven brought a teacher to give an A Plus Certification course. All current Member Connect staff members were forced to participate. I never got the official certification but just being able to say I took the class was enough to impress a few tech support companies. There was one job I applied to that told me I would be starting at sixteen dollars an hour. They also offered incentive bonuses. I could potentially earn up to twenty-three dollars an hour before promotions.

While I loved the idea of making money there was one major issue, I had with every company I applied for. The jobs were too demanding of my time. There was one job where I was told I needed to be there from nine in the morning to six at night six days a week. As much as I enjoy technology, I will never love it. I wanted a career I could actually see myself doing for the next thirty years.

I still wasn't one hundred percent sure what I wanted to do with my life but I know tech wasn't where I wanted to end my journey. I was pissing off some of the higher ups at Haven because there were job opportunities available and I was turning them down.

My mind was already set on going to college. I still wasn't sure of the details but I knew I wanted to pursue a career in the entertainment industry. The only thing I had decided for certain was that I never wanted to sell one of my stories. I hate the idea of spending years of my life crafting an amazing story just to pass it off to a total stranger hoping that he or she won't turn my masterpiece into a flaming pile of garbage.

The summer of 2011 I left my position at Member Connect. I was going to start my first semester of college in the fall and wanted to dedicate myself fully to that. As Member Connect grew it began to take up all of my time. The lab was open morning, noon and night. I've had people come to bed and wake me up because the lab didn't open up on time. Running that program was a full-time job.

The Pell Grant entirely paid for the classes with plenty left over. The first thing I did was go to Best Buy to buy my first laptop. Member Connect put me on the Wi-Fi network. I never went back to the lab after that.

Side note, I noticed something when I bought that laptop. After talking to one of the workers and deciding on the laptop I wanted the girl reached for a box. Then she paused and asked me if I was going to get the Best Buy warranty. When I said no, she put that box back and grabbed a different one. That seems a little suspicious to me. Especially since I only had the laptop a month before it started giving me issues.

Now that I had a laptop, I started using the webcam to record videos and upload them to YouTube. I've had a channel for years where I watch videos. In 2011 I created two new channels where I still regularly upload videos to this day. One of those channels is NathanLyleOfficial where I upload vlogs, sketches, reviews and anything else that catches my fancy. Feel free to go subscribe if you're not already. You can also follow me on Twitter under the same name.

CHAPTER 20

San Antonio College

My first semester at college was nothing like the images I'd grown up seeing in the media. For one thing, I was at a community college. The campus is small. At a leisurely pace it takes about seven minutes to walk from one end to another. Teenagers were the smallest percentage of the population. Most of the students here have jobs and children. Half the time the teacher would be younger than many of the students.

I was hoping to write this book entirely from memory but my years of college have all blended together. Luckily, I still have assignments from every single class. I looked at the dates on those papers to see when I took each class. The five classes I took my first semester were English, Math, History, Sociology and Student Development.

Student Development is required for all first-time students at the school. It's a one credit course so I was only there for a month. It's a class I'm glad I was forced to take. It helped me learn which classes are generally held in which buildings and some of the different services are available to students.

Considering the fact that you're reading a book I wrote you might find it at least slightly surprising that I took a remedial English class. Especially since I entered college as an English major. When I applied to college, I took an exam. I was in that room for less than ten minutes. My scores in math and science were above average. My English scores were abysmal. In this class I learned the reason why.

I wrote my exam essay in just a few minutes. I didn't bother editing myself at all. The two things I lacked most were patience and attention to detail. The main thing I learned from this class was to carefully read through everything I write for even the smallest mistakes. The best thing about this class was that the teacher only gave us a few assignments. Once those were completed, we didn't have to go back. I spent the same amount of time in that class that I did in student development.

The sociology course was by far my favorite. Enjoying the subject made it easier to study. When the teacher was handing back our very first test, he said that in all of his classes only one person got a 100. One by one he would call our names and we'd go to the front of the class to grab our papers.

As I was walking to the front of the class, he stated that I had the highest grade of any student who took this class. He handed me my paper and I saw the 100 at the top of the page. It's the happiest I've ever been about getting a good grade. The lowest grade I ever received in that class was 96.

My least favorite class was easily math. Before I signed up for the class, I looked up the teacher on that Rate My

Professor website. He was rated highly. Most of the reviews said that if you just do the work it would be easy to pass.

When I took the class, I noticed he had a strange way of teaching. He taught us one subject, then a second, then we took a test on the first subject. Then we'd spent two weeks learning a third subject. Then our second test would be over the stuff we learned just before the first test.

I nearly missed the final exam. I came this close to just sleeping through it. I set my alarm for the wrong time. I thought the test was starting at noon but it was at eleven. I woke up ten minutes before the test was supposed to start. I threw some clothes on and ran to school. The college was only a few miles from Haven so a leisurely walk normally took half an hour. I cut that I half when I run.

I walked in the door in the door huffing, puffing and covered in sweat. Everyone was already taking their test. The teacher handed me my test. I sat down and pulled out a pencil. It took about ten minutes to finish. Doubtful of my own skills I triple checked every single problem just to be certain. I didn't notice any mistakes but I just didn't want to believe it could be that easy. I not only passed that class I aced it. I aced every class. I finished my first semester of college with a 4.0 GPA.

During the first days of the semester SAC held welcome days. Every organization in the school sets up booths and tries to recruit members. On the second day of the semester I walked by the KSYM booth. I wasn't aware that there is a radio station operating out of the school. The radio station was in the Radio, Television and Film (RTF) building, which I hadn't known existed before I talked to the people at the booth.

It's hidden away in the back corner of the school. Barely even on the campus. I went there just to check it out. That building would end up becoming my favorite place on campus. I would spend every second of free time there. Well, at least from nine to five. I'd wake up, go to classes then go to the station. I'd always screen one or two albums just to say I was doing something but I spent more time just hanging with cool people or watching YouTube videos.

Towards the end of the first semester I was contacted by the SAHA (San Antonio Housing Authority) representatives on Haven's campus. My Pell Grant counted as income. For fifty dollars a month I could have a private room. It was amazing. I actually had a door I could close to keep the assholes away from me. The bathrooms had actual stalls. I finally got to use a normal shower head again.

The only negative thing was that I kept locking myself out. It took a while to get used to having a door again. Now that I did have that door to keep the rest of the world away, I didn't feel the need to go to KSYM as much. I'd still pop in from time to time to say hi to some of my friends but I never stuck around for long.

CHAPTER 21

Leaving Haven

I expected my new life to be more relaxing than the previous one. It went the opposite direction. The moment I moved into the room the people at Haven started breathing down my neck. They wanted me to move out as soon as possible. At the very least, they wanted to know I was working towards moving out. When the next semester started, I took night classes in order to accommodate their desires.

I took another English course this semester. My teacher's name is difficult to pronounce and impossible to spell so I'll call him Dr. V. Taking his class is one of the best decisions I've ever made. His teaching method was unique. He told us from the very beginning that he would tell us exactly what we needed to know. All we had to do was follow his instructions and we are guaranteed an A in the class.

The other night class I took was history. I was one of the only people in there who hadn't taken this teacher the previous year. It's not that strange for me. I'm used to not being part of the crowd. The only thing I remember about the class was writing a ten-page essay.

The teacher gave us a list of available topics. Of all the subjects on the list I chose prohibition. I figured it would be easy to fill ten pages since that's the subject I already knew the most about. I fell a page and a half short and decided to fill the empty space with unnecessary backstory on the early history of prohibition efforts in the first two hundred years of American history. The teacher saw right through my tactic and directly called me out on it. I still managed to get an A- so I guess I still did a decent job on the other eight pages.

The only other class I had that semester was a biology class I took Saturday mornings. It was supposed to be an all-day event. Class from nine to noon, a one-hour lunch break then lab from one to four. If I remember correctly, we were never in that room past eleven. Most mornings we'd be there for about an hour before she let us go home. I'm not sure how I managed to pass the class. I barely paid attention in class and didn't turn in many of my assignments. I wasn't that concerned with my GPA this semester.

Monday through Friday I spent at least one hour every day looking for jobs online. I had to do that much just to keep the people at Haven of my back. The biggest deterrent to me finding a job is the same problem I have with life in general… people suck.

The majority of applications I put in never got any sort of response. The ones that did respond were far too demanding of my time. I had no choice but to turn them down because I was already invested in attending college. Money is great. Happiness is better.

More than halfway through the semester and I still hadn't found a job. As long as I could show that I was putting in the effort Haven wouldn't hassle me. With that in mind, I wasn't trying as hard as I could. Then I caught an unfortunate break.

There was a person in the job program who had been trying to help me with very little success. One day someone called her with a job opening for a dishwasher and she sent me. If I could've made up some excuse on the spot I would've. My brain doesn't work that fast.

The restaurant, Luke, was only a few blocks from Haven. Took about half an hour to walk there. It was a two-story restaurant attached to a fourteen-story hotel. I walked in the door and the hostess asked if I had a reservation. I told her I was there for a job and she asked me to have a seat and wait.

I sat at the table closest to the door and tried to stay as quiet and motionless as possible. After a while a man called Moose came in and was directed towards me. He walked me around the restaurant for about an hour explaining things about the restaurant and my job duties. He told me my first shift would be tomorrow morning at seven.

The next morning, I showed up fifteen minutes early. Moose never told me the code to open the door. I sat there waiting for someone to show up and let me in. The other morning guys were fifteen minutes late. They showed me step by step the things I had to do before we opened.

We start by taking all the clean plates upstairs to restock the kitchen before the cooks show up. Then we sweep and mop the dining room downstairs. Then we start washing any leftover dishes from last night. By the time we get through those more dirty dishes have usually arrived.

Like most things in life the job was scary at first but I quickly got the hang of it. My first day there I met the head chef. I wanted to know my schedule. He showed me where they kept the schedules then scratched out somebody's name and wrote mine. I told him I couldn't work Saturday so he scratched it out and wrote me back in on Sunday.

I don't remember the exact date but early on I had to work a double. Have you ever spent sixteen straight hours standing at a sink scrubbing pots and pans? Thanks to that day I worked over fifty hours that week. It was the biggest paycheck of my life.

The good news is that my bank account was steadily growing. The bad news is that it didn't ease the pressure. I thought that getting a job would quiet the noise for at least a little bit. Instead, Haven started pushing even harder. As soon as I started the job, they started trying to force me out.

Does that sound smart to you? Get a job and use your entire first paycheck to get an apartment? That's not a great idea. Especially since I already used my first paycheck to buy a handheld camera and tripod so that I could upload higher quality videos to YouTube.

I also bought a four-hundred-dollar smart phone. There was this promotion that Verizon did with Dominos where they gave away free smart phones. They wouldn't give me one because I had no credit history. I was told that if I paid the four hundred dollars up front as a security deposit, they would give it back after a year of paying my bills on time and in full.

They did technically give it back. The four hundred dollars appeared in my account. Then for some reason that no one at customer support could explain the money was taken right back out later that same day. You still owe me four hundred dollars Verizon.

Even though Haven was breathing down my neck my contract with SAHA protected me. At least it would have if I decided to fight back. I wanted to leave Haven almost as much as Haven wanted me to leave.

It took a few months before I could find an apartment that would accept me. I didn't make that much money at work and had no credit history. The only reason I was finally able to find a place is because there was staff at Haven specifically to help ease people back into the real world.

I've been told that very few people receive the same benefits as I did. Haven paid the first three month's rent for me and gave me a one-hundred-dollar H.E.B. gift card. The woman in charge of the private rooms tried to get me to reconsider.

My rent at Haven was fifty dollars a month. My new apartment would cost nearly five hundred dollars a month. I could save thousands of dollars by waiting out my contract and getting the S.A.H.A. housing voucher.

I liked the idea of saving a ton of money. I loved the idea of leaving Haven more. The day I signed the lease I spent the night in the empty apartment. No furniture or food. Not even a blanket.

They gave me the key and I spent the night sprawled out on the kitchen floor. I latched onto my neighbor's Wi-Fi and watched YouTube videos until I passed out. That was the most relaxing sleep of my life.

CHAPTER 22

I'm An Adult?

The day after I got my key I went to Haven and emptied out my room. Back then everything I owned fit in one large box. Did I forget to mention that the apartments I moved into were just down the street from Haven? Well, at least it wasn't right next to the train tracks. It's so much easier to get a full night of sleep when you don't have a train going past your window at three in the morning. Even if you're lying on the floor because you didn't have furniture that first week you lived there.

The second week that I lived there, on a Friday morning, a couple of people who worked at Haven's warehouse brought a bunch of stuff to fill my apartment. I am eternally grateful to the people who picked everything out. They brought me a couch, a recliner and a huge TV. They also brought a ton of pots, pans, plates and silverware. So much more than I'll ever need. There are about twenty plates and bowls that have spent seven years just sitting on a shelf.

Getting comfortable in my new apartment was surprisingly difficult. I was so excited to leave Haven that it felt like heaven at first. Then a few issues started popping up. For the first time in my life I was entirely self-dependent. In my first month I spent over eight hundred dollars on pizza.

That might sound like a joke but I'm completely serious. I ordered pizza. I ate pizza. I ordered more pizza. At the end of the month I added all my receipts together and realized that I'm an adult now. I need to make better decisions. From that point on I made sure to keep a budget. I'd only allow myself to spend a certain amount of money each month and kept track of where every single cent went.

Living alone was scary and fun at the same time. I can wake up whenever I want. Go to sleep whenever I want. I don't have to wear clothes if I'm not going outside. For the first time in my life I can masturbate without fear that someone might barge in. This is also the first time in my life that I didn't have a bed.

Most nights I would sleep on the recliner. I also got a huge floral comforter. I didn't know what to do with it so I threw it over the couch. I figured that when it got dirty, I could take that off and throw it into the wash. It would be much easier than cleaning the couch itself. How do you even clean a couch?

Cleaning is the one adjustment I've struggled with the most. I'm a very messy person. There could be various reasons why. Have I learned to detest cleaning because of the slave-like labor I endured in my childhood? Or is it simply a fact of life that some people just don't care about cleanliness? Very likely a combination of both.

At the end of the day I just don't care enough about appearances to give any consistent effort. This is my place. You don't like it you can leave. I shouldn't have to adjust my living environment to suit other people. The person that should be the most comfortable here is me.

This mindset has some unfortunate side effects. After a few months in the apartment I was contacted by SAHA about having my rent reduced. It never went through. The main reason... my apartment was never clean enough. I think people need to be educated on the difference between clean and organized. I consider my place to be clean because there's nothing on the floor. Apparently, the word clean means it needs to look like a display home.

I'll never be able to make a place that I live in look so good that you wonder whether or not someone actually lives there. After a few tries I gave up. For the second time that year I threw away a chance to save thousands of dollars. I'll only clean my apartment three times a year when the managers comes in to do maintenance or pest control.

One of the best things about living alone was that I could watch whatever I want whenever I want. I can watch WNBA games without hearing some idiot constantly complaining "They can't even dunk." I can watch PBS without people judging me. I know I'm a weirdo. It still doesn't feel good to be looked at like I'm an alien. Most importantly I can watch all the anime I want. That year I saw a commercial for The Devil is a Part Timer and thought it seemed interesting. The story was hilarious and I got hooked easily. That's the first time I ever followed a simulcast show.

The most difficult thing about my new life was my job. Even once I got used to the daily expectations, I still struggled to fulfill the role. Mostly because I didn't have too many great coworkers. I'm easily the best dishwasher that restaurant has ever had.

That's mostly because I'm one of the only people to give that kind of effort. The majority of dishwashers were just there to earn an easy paycheck. They do the bare minimum then go home. I was the only dishwasher who was great at his job that never got promoted into the kitchen.

There was an endless parade of subpar coworkers that I could describe. There was one guy who hardly ever showed up for any his shifts. The few times that he actually was there he barely did any work at all. Yet he never stopped complaining about how hard his job was and how lazy the other dishwashers were.

He only held onto the job for so long because we were shorthanded. Once we reached four dishwashers on our morning staff he was let go. He wasn't even the worst dishwasher we've ever had. There was once a seventeen-year-old on probation who consistently showed up to work stoned off his ass and was fired when a flask full of liquor fell out of his pocket.

Near the end of summer, I asked to be moved to the night shift so I could have my days free to return to my normal college life. The night shift took some time to get used to. It was a different set of people and a much busier shift.

The night dishwashers weren't as horrible as I thought. They sucked…but it's not like they didn't give any effort. When I first arrived the first floor was the place to be. There's a giant machine doing most of the work and chef isn't breathing down your neck.

That's why I hated letting the others work downstairs. It was easier for them to get away with being lazy. I'd rather they stay upstairs where they're actually forced to work. It took some time but eventually we reached the point where the machine downstairs became known as my station. Once that point was reached the upstairs suddenly became the best hangout spot. That's how my life has always been. The best place to be is wherever I'm not.

I switched my major at college. I was trying for an Associates of Arts for Radio and Television Broadcasting and an Associates of Applied Science for Media Convergence and Production. Since many of those classes overlapped, I decided it would be worth going for both. It would only take one or two additional semesters to get through the extra classes. I had tried to frontload on the unnecessary classes like math, history and science so that the last things I learned in school were all necessary to my degree.

Quick reminder of where I am in my life at this point in the book. A twenty-two-year-old with a full-time job beginning his third semester of college. I barely had an idea in my head of what I might want to do with my life when I grow up. I was working for eight dollars an hour and fighting to get as many hours as possible.

Most months I would earn less than a thousand dollars. Thank god for college. I wouldn't have survived without it. Lesson number one children: Apply for everything. Even if you know you don't qualify you should still apply. You never know when you'll get lucky and there will be an accounting error.

Every year I would get multiple grants and scholarships. One of them would entirely pay for classes and books while the rest would go into my bank account. That bank account was the proudest thing in my life. The numbers continued to rise. I remember a very specific moment when I checked the balance and proudly proclaimed "It's over 9000!" It helps that I lived a boring life. I had no romantic partners or kids. I didn't smoke, drink or own a car. Most of the people I met could check off two or three things on that list. A few of them could check off all five.

That semester I tried to schedule all my classes for Tuesdays and Thursdays so I wouldn't have to work on days I went to school. I took an English class at eight in the morning. I greatly regret that. If you're not a morning person you should never take morning classes.

Since class started at eight, I had to be out my door by 7:30 at the latest. Which means I had to be awake by seven at the latest if I wanted to shower and eat breakfast. This was incredibly difficult since most nights I wouldn't get home from work till one in the morning.

The teacher was far too nice. I should've failed that class. I skipped classes often enough I'm shocked she didn't just remove me from the class roster. When I did show up I had trouble keeping my eyes open. I didn't even attempt half of the reading assignments. My grades should've been abysmal. Yet somehow at the end of the semester I had a passing grade.

The class I had right after English was Speech. It was one of the most fun classes I've ever had. Partly because by the time the class started, I'd finally woken up. Some days I was one chocolate bar away from leading the entire class in a performance of I Want It That Way. I'm very thankful for that.

I've always had a problem with public speaking. There's nothing I hate more than being the focus of attention. I prefer to stay in the background where no one notices me. So it was a great benefit to take this class while experiencing a natural high.

When I think back to that semester those are the only two classes I can remember clearly. I took my final math class that semester. I took Intro to Mass Communications because it was required for my degree. I also took Writing for Radio, Television and Film. It seemed like a good place to start since it might be a potential career for me. Plus, my degree advisor was teaching that class so I thought it was a good idea for us to familiarize ourselves with each other.

Everything Is Impossible

CHAPTER 23

Things Change

The thing about working any job is that there can be a lot of turnover. That's the biggest change from life as a student to life in the real world. Elementary school through college I could always count on seeing the same people over and over again until the year is over.

At a paying job you can never be sure when this is the last time you'll see someone. Many people get fired or quit with no notice. At one point our head chef left. It felt identical to high school when we got the new band directors. This new leader was much more relaxed.

A new girl named Crystal started working at Luke. She was my height with peach skin, brown eyes, chubby cheeks and blonde hair. The first thing most people noticed about her were the huge boobs. The moment she walked in the door every guy at the restaurant asked for her phone number. I wanted no part of that circus.

I'm not sure how we became friends. One day she approached me and started talking. We slowly became friends and she would regularly give me rides home after work. On New Year's Eve the restaurant stayed open till midnight. We clocked out at one in the morning. Crystal drove me home, stopping by Jack in the Box to buy a munchie meal for us to share. I ate most of it while she just snacked on a few fries.

I'm not sure how we got into this position but for some reason she was leaning against me. The back of her head was resting on my chest and my arms were wrapped around her stomach. Earlier that night Crystal had asked me to be her midnight kiss. I laughed it off and kept working. Now here we are at two in the morning sitting in the front seat of her car with tired legs, full stomachs and 98 Degrees playing on the speaker. Next thing I know are lips are touching.

I'd call it a make out session but that's not entirely accurate. I pressed my lips against hers. We'd sit there motionless for a few minutes. She'd pull her lips away. I'd lean in again. We kept repeating this process for about twenty minutes before she told me she had to go home and make sure her dogs are fine. I went to my apartment and took a cold shower then spanked the monkey for two hours until I fell asleep.

That night ruined our friendship. Crystal once told me that the reason she wanted to talk to me as because I ignored her. Every guy in the restaurant hit on her the moment she walked in the door. I pretended she didn't exist.

She was excited to get to know me because she knew that I didn't want anything from her. So if I started liking her it meant that my feelings were genuine. After that night I couldn't look at her without thinking about sex. Sorry to disappoint you Crystal. Turns out I'm just like everyone else. A few months later she left the restaurant and we immediately lost touch.

There's a reason I remember that day so vividly. That's the last time I kissed a girl. I've kissed five females in my life. They've all been so few and far between that they're all easy to remember. When I was five a teacher at my daycare held me down so a girl who had a crush on me could give me a kiss. She kissed me and I kicked her face.

Then there was my high school girlfriend. She's the only one who ever used tongue. It happened the last two times we made out. Then there was Valentine's Day 2011 when I made out with Abby and got a peck on the lips from Sandy.

Then there was Crystal on New Year's Day 2013. I'm turning twenty-nine this month and I've had less than ten minutes of sex in my life, which happened seventeen years ago, and maybe an hour of kissing, the last of which happened six years ago. I'm reaching that point where I jizz my pants every time a woman looks at me.

When my fourth semester of college started, I had a full course load. I don't think I got more than three total hours of sleep that semester. I had one early morning class. The official title was Music Appreciation but as my teacher liked to say it was more music history. My teacher was a young guy. The first time I saw him I thought he was one of the students.

He told us this was only his second semester as a teacher. He loved going to college so much that he decided to stay forever. In this class we learned the exact definition of what music is and full history of music starting with Gregorian chants. Turns out the class name is accurate. I gained a much greater appreciation of music after taking the class. My music taste broadened to include everything from renaissance to dubstep.

When that class ended, I went to the RTF building for TV Production One. It would make more sense to call it studio production. I don't remember the teacher's name but I'd been warned about taking his class. Unfortunately, it was a degree requirement and he was the only one teaching it that semester.

Day one the class was split in half and those were our teams for the rest of the semester. Our first homework assignment was to write a thirty second commercial. It could be for any product we choose. We would shoot it live on a three-camera set.

I chose to write a commercial for Suave for men liquid soap. Since I was using that brand at the time, I could buy a bunch of bottles as props then when we finish, I can just take them home. Since my script was chosen, I got to be the director and operate the switchboard.

Most of us had relatively easy jobs. I just stared at monitors and pushed buttons. Two of the three cameras we set the shot and they just held them in place. Our actor, Jeff, had the most difficult job. He had to memorize all his lines and which camera he says each line into. All while wearing a bathrobe. He did an amazing job.

The only thing I hated about that project was Felicity, our floor manager. She had a bad habit of disregarding the things I say and giving her own orders. On our last day of the project we did a run through and it was perfect. There wasn't a single complaint. Then, completely unbeknownst to anyone else, she tells camera one to tilt up.

I didn't notice it until the middle of filming. I wanted to tell him the corrections but I was too afraid. This was the real deal. I'd rather be stuck on a bad shot than to have one or more shots where the camera is moving. That horrible shot in the final product lowered our grades and I developed a permanent hatred for Felicity.

Our next project was a PSA about drunk driving. I worked camera two. For an entire month my job was just zooming in on pictures of car wrecks on a poster board. Or third project was the last bit of fun I had in this class. We were filming a promotional video for the RTF program at our school and we get the chance to use green screen. I wrote a fun script and we combined it with the informative script that Jeff wrote.

I wanted to star in the commercial because I've always wanted to be on a green screen. There was another guy in the group who wanted to star in the commercial as well so we held auditions. I performed much better. They chose the other guy. Though it was never said out loud I strongly believe that the final decision was influenced by the massive cut on my face. I was told that it made me look even scarier than usual.

That cut was given to me buy a coworker named Patrick. He had some very obvious mental deficits and we all tried to be considerate of that. There were days when he made that impossible. This day was especially difficult.

At my station there were these metal bars above my head. Resting on those bars were racks that we'd put the dirty drinking glasses into. On that day Patrick decided that he couldn't be bothered to pour the drinks out of the cups before putting them in the rack. He kept splashing me all night and I was getting frustrated. I kept telling him to stop and his response was always "stop crying. It's just water."

That's when it happened. Patrick came through and poured water on me again. I had a fork in my hand. I tossed it at him. It bounced lightly off his chest. Didn't leave a single mark on his jacket. It made him angry. He ran at me with his arms flailing.

I wanted to punch him. I wanted to make him bleed. I also wanted to keep paying rent. I wanted to keep eating pizza. I knew that if I threw a single punch I would be fired. So I grabbed him, put him in a headlock and took him to the ground. I had him pinned but he kept trying to grab my face.

There was another guy there when it happened. He ran out of the room to grab a manager. After I took Patrick down a runner walked in the room and told us to chill. I told him that I was ok. Patrick is the one who needed to calm down. I stood up and walked to the back of the room.

Patrick stood up and tried to run for me again but the runner stood between us and held Patrick back. After a few seconds Patrick gave up and left the room. From what I understand he walked out the front door and went home. I went back to work and acted like nothing had happened.

I didn't work the next day. I was told Patrick showed up and was immediately sent away. Since I wasn't there people thought we had both been fired. I double checked with the manager just to be sure. I wasn't fired but I did have to sit through a small lecture.

I didn't even realize I was injured. Someone pointed out to me that I had a cut on my cheek. It wasn't deep. There was no blood. I felt no pain but the cut stayed there for a while. Even if it wasn't one hundred percent the reason, I didn't get the role it definitely played a part. On the positive side my group ended up rewriting parts of the script and I was given a voiceover role.

For the final project the two groups joined together for a music video. We filmed a woman singing a Nora Jones song while playing he harp. My official role was the b-roll assistant. The main b-roll guy handled it so well that I had nothing to do. I filled in at cameraman once when someone was sick but for the majority of the project, I was one of three people that sat around doing absolutely nothing.

The most upsetting thing about that was Felicity. She was made floor manager despite my warnings. The main reason they gave her the role is because she seemed to want it so much. That's a horrible reason to give someone a job. Wanting it more doesn't guarantee she'll be better at it.

She kept pulling the same bullshit that she did in the first project. Disregarding the director to give her own personal opinions on what the camera operators should do. There were a few specific examples where she told them the exact opposite of what the director said. Despite this turmoil we somehow managed to film a good video. The teacher had the smuggest look on his face. It disgusted me. He gave himself too much credit.

I only passed the class because I cheated. Before the semester began every single one of us had been warned that he gives you the same test for his finals that he does for the midterm. What we didn't count on was how difficult the midterm would be.

Only one person passed. It was the kid we called Spielberg. He's that kid. You know the one. The guy who had the entire text book memorized a week before classes started. Even he could barely manage to pass with a 72. That was the highest score in the entire class.

Two other people studied their butts off and managed to get 60s. The majority of us were scoring in the 20s and 30s. The teacher was pissed off about that. He tried to claim that he gave us a comprehensive review. Those words pissed us off so much. His "comprehensive review" was just to spend one class period flipping through the pages of this 1000-page book and state the things we were expected to know. You remember Ben Stein in Ferris Bueller's Day Off? That's basically what this guy sounded like. Teacher: "Chroma key...Blah blah...blah blah...*flips page*...blah blah...blah blah."

When he gave us back the graded papers he went over the exam, giving us the answer to every single question. We were writing down every word he said knowing full well we had the secret to getting a perfect score on our final exam. Then he asked for the tests back.

Luckily, one person in the class was smart enough to take a picture and send it to all of us. During the final exam I pulled out my phone when the teacher wasn't looking and slid it under my exam paper.

Everyone in the class got an A on the final exam. When he handed back the graded test, we all tried our best to fake a shocked reaction. In my opinion we failed horribly but he seemed fooled. I mean seriously, how long have you been teaching? Do you think none of your students have ever talked? It's not a well-guarded secret.

If any administrators are thinking of revoking my credit for that class, you'll probably have to do it for 85% of the people who have taken that man's class. Yet here he is giving us that smug smile. Patting himself on the back for how great a job he did teaching us.

The only lesson I learned from his class is that there are difficult people in every industry. Whether they be filmmakers or teachers there are always people that just don't deserve their jobs. From what I heard that was his final semester teaching. We like to joke about how we were such a horrible class that he'd rather quit than to ever deal with students like us again.

I had two other RTF class: Media Literacy and Intro to Advertising. After reading through my old assignments I remember some of the things I did in those classes. Then I remembered that I wanted to write this book entirely from memory. So I won't talk about them. This chapter is long enough already. So long that I've decided to take the other class I took that semester and put it in its own separate chapter.

Chapter 24

Creative Writing

Creative Writing was easily the greatest part of my entire college experience. I'm not just saying that because I plan on showing this book to my teacher from that class. I honestly enjoyed this class more than any other I've ever taken in my entire life. There were a few different assignments in the class but the manuscripts were the most important ones. That's what we spent the majority of the semester focused on.

I chose to work on a story that I came up with while at Haven. I decided this class would be a good chance to develop it. We had a twenty-page limit. I wasn't sure if I could fill ten pages. All I had at the time was a two-page document describing each character and their role in the story. I ended up writing thirty pages. I was forced to delete a few things. There were sentences in the middle of conversations being deleted. There were entire scenes getting dropped. I completely deleted two characters.

I still only got down to twenty-five pages. So I changed the format on the pages and started rearranging things in order to squeeze as much of the story into twenty pages as I could. Making the font size smaller is out of the question.

That's the first thing teachers look at. The editing continued. With the deadline nearing I was forced to turn in this incredibly stripped-down version that was essentially still a rough draft.

The biggest issue laying ahead was that I had to print a twenty-page manuscript for every person in my class. We had over twenty students which meant I would be printing over 400 pages. Printing on campus cost ten cents a page. That means the total cost of printing all these manuscripts would be over forty dollars. I overheard a classmate saying she got hers printed at the UPS store on campus. I decided to check it out.

It was definitely much cheaper but still not free. Every copy I printed cost me money so you can understand why I was upset when I gave every single person in that class a manuscript and less than half of the gave me a review. Then again, I also understand why.

It may have only been twenty pages but it was an overstuffed intense emotional drama and you only have a week to read it in the middle of the semester. I had a full-time job and was taking five classes that semester. If anyone handed me something more than ten pages, I simply skimmed it once and wrote down my first impression.

The most difficult thing about the class was the roundtable discussions. Every time we read a manuscript, we arrange the desk in a circle. We spend the entire class tearing the stories to shreds. It was easier with some stories than others.

There were three different people in the class who wrote an absolutely horrible story. The only thing I wanted to tell them was "You are not a writer. Please drop this class." The teacher told us we had to be constructive in our criticism. I tried my best to give advice on what I would do to improve the story.

When my story was being reviewed it was nerve-racking. While I appreciate getting feedback on the story it also felt like a punishment. I have to sit here listening to people tell me every single thing they hated about my story and I'm not allowed to defend myself.

Half of their criticisms were things I had noticed and didn't have the chance to fix before the due date. There were also things I did purposely that people didn't seem to understand. There was only one person who clearly understood the purpose behind the story. Even the teacher didn't comprehend the message quite as well a she did.

The teacher required us to turn in three manuscripts. The final manuscript must be a drastic rewrite of one of your previous manuscripts. If your second manuscript is a rewrite of your first one that's the story you're stuck with for the rest of the semester.

For my second story I decided to use a spec script I'd written while I was still living at Haven. It was a 107-page script about a teenage superhero. I took the first ten pages and reformatted them. That way I'd have more time to make improvements to my first manuscript. I only worked on the second manuscript during class when the teacher forced us to do writing exercises.

For the final manuscript I skewered the first story down to eight pages and changed the point of view from third person omniscient to first person. I added a few personal touches as well. It was difficult but worthwhile. This new version of the story was far more intimate.

On the last day of the semester we each had to stand in front of the class reading two pages of our new story that show off the rewrites. Most people read two consecutive pages. I read two separate pages. I felt sad when that class finished. If money and free time weren't an issue I'd love to enroll in a fine arts school and get a creative writing degree. This class was my favorite thing about the entire college experience.

CHAPTER 25

Finding a Dream

The next semester at school was my absolute favorite. It was the first, last and only semester where every single one of my classes was in the RTF building. Made my life so much easier not having to run around campus all day. The most difficult class I had that year was Television Field Production taught by Mr. O. Much like everything else in my life the toughest part about it was the people I had to deal with.

For every project we worked on our final assignment was to write a paper telling the teacher what we thought of the project and how well our group members did. I gave a scathing indictment of all my teammates on every project. It's very possible that I was the only one in class who gave an honest review and Mr. O thinks I just don't work well with people. I do work well with others; I just have standards.

The first project was a how-to video. I had a fun idea to make a how-to video about how to make a how-to video. One of the guys in our group, Armando, was supposed to ask Mr. O if the concept was ok. He never did. Upon further analysis I realize I could've asked Mr. O myself if he approved of the concept. At the time, I just didn't stop to think about it. I was so excited to write the script that I dove headfirst into it.

When I emailed my finished script to the others Armando said that I wrote too much. He thought I overestimated how much five minutes was. With help from two of his friends he "rewrote" my script. The only change they made was gutting it like a fish till there was nothing left but the bare minimum.

That pile of garbage they tried to pass off as a script wouldn't fill twenty seconds of footage. My script might have been slightly overstuffed but it's always better to have too much footage and be forced to cut something than to not have enough to fill your time.

Mr. O agreed with me. When Armando showed him the revised script he was crucified for that very fact. It lacked enough substantial content to fill out the required time. On top of that, he told us that he didn't like our video idea. He wanted our how-to video to be something you could physically do.

I told them that if they pick the subject, I'd be happy to write the script. Armando said he didn't want me to write the script because Mr. O hated my first one. How bad is your memory? He never saw my script. He hated that trash you wrote. He only disapproved of my concept.

For the rest of the project I basically did nothing. I was more than willing to help but was constantly being shoved aside and told to not touch anything. Don't know how we got a passing grade. Our final project was barely two and a half minutes long and it wasn't very high quality. There was one guy who took on the entire project himself, refusing to let anyone touch anything, and another who did absolutely nothing yet still gave himself far too much credit. In case you couldn't tell, that last one was Armando.

My next group was much easier to work with. Partly due to the fact that none of them were overly excited about doing any of the hard work. So when I volunteered for different jobs they wouldn't try to stop me. Our first project was an interview. We ran into a major problem when we couldn't figure out the lavalier mic and didn't get good audio. We had to record the interview a second time but other than that one hiccup this project went fairly well.

Our final project in the class was to make a five-minute movie with less than twenty-five words. It was frustrating but I understand the point behind the assignment. Let the video tell the story instead of relying on dialogue to explain what's happening. The group decided on a romantic movie.

I took lead on crafting the story. When we showed it to Mr. O he had plenty of criticisms. We definitely went over the word limit. He kept telling us it wouldn't make sense for the characters not to say anything in some of those situations.

When we first started filming, I was the primary camera operator. Then Leslie got mad at me for taking my time. I wanted to make sure each shot was perfect. I was having difficulty using the tripod but I always got the right shot. Leslie said we needed to hurry up and just get through it. Then we got to editing and she ended up hating more than half of the shots she filmed. We had to reshoot a lot of different scenes.

Another class I took that year was video editing. The thing I enjoyed most about that class was the complete autonomy. Whether I failed or succeeded I did it entirely on my own. I spent most of the class failing. The teacher never gave me a low grade but every project I put together was a nasty mess. More than anything else I was feeling things out while I learned my way around this new world of editing.

A third class I took that year was radio experience. The first half of the year was spent in a classroom just practicing the procedure for being on the radio. Introducing the songs, reading the PSA and the weather report. I also spent the semester shadowing Leslie on her radio show. It was a live show, so once a week I got to watch an in-studio performance and sit in on the interview. During the second half of the semester I spent an hour a week sitting in the KSYM booth as a DJ.

My favorite part of that semester was easily audio production. I'm glad this class was a degree requirement otherwise I never would've taken it. Do you remember Jeff from Television Production One? He was in the audio production class with me. We did three of our projects together. We did Foley for a video, a thirty second radio commercial for transformers and a five-minute mockumentary discussing why modern-day teenagers aren't having enough sex.

The only time I worked alone that year was when we did our radio imaging project. We had to create a fake radio station and make bumpers, commercials, show intros and stingers. I decided to make a radio station entirely for boy bands. The entire process was fun. Recording, editing and creating the perfect sound effects.

I was very proud of the final product I turned it. Best of all, the project being played for the class was the most exhilarating moment of my life. People laughed when I wanted them to laugh. The teacher was impressed by my creativity and skill. It wasn't a standing ovation but it felt like it.

The experiences I had that year helped shape my perspective on things. This led to a life affirming discovery. I finally knew what I wanted to do with the rest of my life. I want to be the next Disney. Not Walt Disney the person. Disney the corporation. That company has TV shows, movies and radio stations. They bought Marvel and Star Wars for Christ's sake.

That's what I want. I want to see my shows on TV. I want to see my movies in theaters. I want to make comic books and video games. I want to set up an office in Japan to make manga and anime. I still don't know how I'll get there but now I finally have an idea for what my end goal in life is. I want to own a multimedia corporation.

Everything Is Impossible

CHAPTER 26

Student Film

There was a bartender I worked with named Hilary. She was a few inches shorter than me. Shoulder length black hair, luscious lips and olive skin. She was already working there when I first began the job. We barely talked at first. When we did talk, we spent every second insulting each other. I'd like to say for the record that she started it. She insulted me and I reacted in kind. I was only trying to fit in to the established culture.

One random day she stopped talking to me. Told me that she didn't feel like talking to a jerk who did nothing but make fun of her. I apologized, even though it was all her fault in the first place, and we started becoming friends. By this point in the story we had gotten really close. I'm talking comfortable enough to discuss masturbation techniques with each other.

When I first realized I was developing feelings for her I kept it to myself. I knew she had a boyfriend because she talked about him all the time. It's been pointed out to me that I have a bad habit of only falling for women who are emotionally unavailable.

At least it's gotten easier to tell whether or not someone is interested in me. I just ask myself this simple question. Is she alive? If the answer is yes then she probably has no interest in dating me. If the answer is no then she probably has no interest in dating me.

Sometime last year, I believe around October, I found out that Hilary and her boyfriend were no longer together. I decided not to say anything. They'd been together for years. She needed time to get over it. I didn't want to be a rebound fling.

At the beginning of February, I asked her if there was any possibility that she might be willing to spend Valentine's Day with me. She said she might consider it if we both got the night off. We were both put on the schedule for Valentine's Day. We were also both on the schedule for the night before.

When we left work that night it was one in the morning and she was giving me a ride home. We were at a red light with Baby Got Back blasting when a cop drove by. He made a U-turn and started flashing his lights. Hilary got upset with me. She was saying, "I can't help but think if I wasn't driving down this road at this time of night..." Then the cop told her that he noticed the date on her sticker had expired. He gave her a warning and told her to get the car inspected. Ha! Not my fault Hilary. Keep your stickers up to date.

Once we got back to my apartment, I asked her to wait for a minute. I ran up to my apartment and went back to her car with a shoebox in my hand. What was in that shoebox you ask? Candy. Lots and lots of candy. As Valentine's Day was approaching, I asked Hilary what type of candy she liked. She said she loved caramel. For the next two weeks I was collecting every type of chocolate I could find that had caramel in it.

I asked her if there was any possibility that she and I could ever be boyfriend and girlfriend. She said she wasn't sure. She then went into detail about the on again off again nature of her relationship with her boyfriend. They've been doing this dance for over eight years. She wasn't sure if she was done with him forever yet.

I took her at her word and never brought it up again. Turns out I forgot one little detail. I'm still me. Soon after, she started dating another guy we work with. A few months later she got a new job and we slowly started to lose touch.

Different date. Different time. Different place. Different girl. Same result. I understand that the majority of the time women do this in a sincere effort to avoid hurting my feelings but it's incredibly misguided. No matter how it happens getting turned down always sucks. From now on can any girl who turns me down please be crass? It would make it easier to get over you.

While that was happening in my personal life, I was also attending my second to last semester of college. I took four classes this semester but I've decided to only talk about the most significant one. In my three years at college the most meaningful class I took was Film Style

Production taught by Donnie Meals. It was a class you could only take after you've already done the majority of classes on the degree plan.

The entire semester was spent working on a single project. A short film no longer than fifteen minutes. When the semester first began Donnie asked the class a question. Do we want the entire class to work on a single project together or should we split up into small groups? I chose to vote for small groups. If we have multiple projects that makes it more likely that I'd be able to bring one of my own stories to life.

We held a vote and small groups won. There were twelve people in the class so we would be divided into four groups of three. Then we were given our first assignment. Write down ten story ideas. We'd bring them to class and vote on the ones we like the most. I was one of only three people to turn in more than one page. Mine was five pages long. The majority of people turned in a single paper with nothing but ten sentences on it.

The teacher took time to read all our ideas to the class and we voted on our favorites. The top four vote earners would be the stories we spent the rest of the semester working on. After the first round there were some ties. The most voted stories were removed from the list and the remainders were voted on again.

They say it's an honor just to be nominated. Bull. I was this close. One vote. That was the difference between directing my first movie and being part of someone's crew.

I was so mad that I stood up and stormed out of the room. For a moment I considered dropping the class and trying again next year.

I convinced myself to walk back in the room. Then I had both salt and lemon poured into my wound. The four people whose stories were chosen got to pick their two helpers. The guy whose story beat mine, Sean, chose me to be on his team. I wrote a two-paragraph summary. He wrote one sentence. The one good thing about the situation is the fact that his story was barely an idea. I volunteered to write the script so I could make it my own.

Things were not going well. Every step of the way we had major issues. We were the last ones to film. Other people had the script written and started recording immediately. It took us months to perfect the script. By perfect, I mean time was running short and we had to film something.

We started filming after spring break. I had taken my vacation time from work in order to be present for every second of filming. Then we fell a week behind on finalizing the script. Luckily my free time coincided well with other people's work schedules.

We contacted a teacher in the theater department about having a casting call for actors. We got permission to use the TV studio for auditions but no one showed up. Two of the actors we ended up with were Sean's friends who decided to help out. The third actor was a guy we brought in to help with audio and create the soundtrack. We started filming before that role had been filled and we just asked him if he wanted to step in.

We mostly filmed around campus. We got permission to film a couple of scenes in the library. We spent an entire day filming in the Tobin Lofts, a brand-new apartment building on campus for the students. They let us use a display room for the main character's apartment.

We filmed one scene in the campus courtyard. One scene was filmed in front of some random house just off campus. The rest of the scenes were filmed in different places throughout the RTF building. There were times when it was fun and times when it was frustrating but for the most part filming went smoothly. We only had to do reshoots once and we took care of it fairly quickly.

We had difficulties getting the footage off the camera. I can't explain the technical aspects very well. Something went wrong with the memory card so we had to use the backup tape that was in the camera. In order to use the footage off the tape we had to render it in real time which took us hours. On top of that it took a few tries for us to get it right.

One day we were still in the middle of this process when Donnie was absent. I decided to leave campus and go home. Halfway there I started getting texts from my group members about why I wasn't there so I turned around and headed back. I lied and told them I just stepped out for lunch. I didn't need to be there. We literally spent the entire afternoon just staring at a screen.

Once we had all our footage then came the editing. That might've been the easiest part of the entire process. We had all the footage we needed and knew exactly what to do with it. We didn't need too many effects. Just put the footage into the timeline in the right order. The most difficult part was sound mixing which Sean handled. My final contribution to the project was making a blooper reel.

At the end of the semester every group screened their finished film for the class to watch. Donnie was shocked at how well we did. He wasn't sure if we'd be able to finish the project because of how dysfunctional we were. That turned out to be our saving grace.

We spent so much time arguing. We spent way too much time on the script. We started editing a week before the deadline. We were the only group with a video longer than five minutes.

One of the groups backed themselves into a corner. They filmed for two days and were never able to get back to the location. They spent the next two months editing. The end result was an impressive looking video with a difficult to follow storyline. Even the people who wrote the story had trouble following their own video.

Despite having the most trouble throughout the process our group had the best final project. There was a screening for all our films. From what I understand no one in my group showed up. We all had to work that night.

Everything Is Impossible

CHAPTER 27

Leaving Luke

Have you seen the Pixar movie Inside Out? I have no plans to ever watch it. I can't even watch the commercials without getting pissed off. I can't say the movie is bad without watching it. It's a cool concept and it might be very well made. There are just some things I can't get over.

First of all, not every human on the planet is entirely ruled by emotions. We all feel emotions but each of us processes them differently. Many people are actually capable of rational thought.

Secondly, not everybody feels the exact same emotions. Disgust is not one of my core emotions. Even though I have money now I still eat things out of the trash can sometimes. You won't believe how many people throw away perfectly good food.

Joy definitely isn't my primary emotion. My primary emotion is Pain. He's the offspring of Sadness and Anger. He's married to doubt. She's the adopted daughter of Fear and Insecurities. Together the two of them run the heart.

Have you ever seen a movie called Osmosis Jones? Ever since watching that as a kid I've imagined all the little people in my body controlling me. There are four main powers that control the Nation of Nathan: body, heart, mind and soul.

Body is very simple. What do we need right now? Brain is currently ruled by Forethought. Soul is split between three people: The Angel, the Devil and a mediator to deliver the final verdict.

I need to take a second to briefly talk about my stance on good versus evil since people keep getting the wrong idea in their head anytime I bring up the subject of good versus evil. I do not believe morality is a static thing. Everyone has their own personal opinion of what is right and what is wrong.

I firmly believe that the only difference between good and evil is which side of the line you're standing on. You might be looking at someone thinking that you're absolutely right and they're absolutely wrong. Meanwhile, they might be looking at you thinking the exact same thing.

As A child the body controlled every choice I made. If the body said it was hungry then I ate. If the body was tired then I rested. The body got five votes while everyone else got one. Then I became a teenager. The heart started gaining more and more power. Joy never ruled my heart. Hope did.

Hope kept telling me to take chances. Kept telling me to ask that girl out. The more power she gained the more she made decisions without consulting anyone. The decisions she made kept causing Nathan more heartache so the citizens grew tired of her. She was impeached. Not only was she removed from office she was locked in a box and hidden away in a storage shed.

Once Pain and Doubt took over, they worked overtime trying to restore the citizens' faith in the heart. The damage was already done. By the time I turned twenty the Heart had already lost most of its power. It started around the time I took over as Program Manager of Member Connect. Brain was finally able to take control of The Nation of Nathan. The citizens were tired of tyrannical rule so Brain was not able to take complete control. He did have the deciding vote.

Heart has half a vote, Body and Soul have one vote each while Brain has two votes. It's not technically a dictatorship but there are very few times when Brain gets overruled. In order to keep Brain from getting his way Body, Heart and Soul would all have to agree. It can be very difficult to get three separate entities to agree on anything. Especially since half the time Soul just doesn't bother voting. At most Brain would only have to convince one of the three to agree with him. Heart is the most easily manipulated. As easy as playing a song.

> "Foolish Heart, heed my warning
> You've been wrong before.
> Don't be wrong anymore."
> — Steve Perry. *Foolish Heart.*

This time was different. The entire council was present. Body has been saying for over a year how much he hates this job. Being on his feet for ten hours a day wears Nathan down. Not to mention the allergic reaction to the chemicals constantly giving him rashes. No one likes a rash on their groin. Heart hated this place as well. It just wasn't worth it. There was nothing gratifying about this job.

Those two had been arguing for a while. Brain kept overruling them. We were saving money just in case but do we have enough? How long can we actually last? Will we actually be able to find a better job? We've tried before and failed. I should mention that even though Doubt helps run the heart she's also one of Brain's top advisors.

I planned on giving some sort of notice that I was going to leave my job to focus on finishing college and impressing at my internship but I never got around to telling anyone because I was too afraid to actually commit to quitting. Then one day I found myself hiding on the balcony. I was sitting in a corner, pressing myself into the wall with my knees pulled up to my chest. I sat there for ten minutes. I spent five of those minutes bawling.

That's when Soul finally decided to take a side. He chose to agree with Heart and Body. Nathan can't keep working at Luke. It'll lead him to suicide. With Soul casting his vote Brain had two options. Option number one is to accept defeat. Option number two was to use his emergency veto. He'd never used it before. Not just because he didn't need it; because it was dangerous.

With the emergency veto you can get exactly what you want. The drawback is that you're guaranteed to lose your power. If you ignore the wishes of every single citizen in The Nation of Nathan and just do what you want you stand to lose all of their respect and could soon find yourself ousted. That's exactly what happened to Hope.

Brain made the decision to ignore his personal desires for the sake of maintaining control. He accepted his loss and temporarily ceded power to the heart. I went the rest of the night business as usual. Before I clocked out, I told seven different people that I had no intention of returning tomorrow.

They all laughed like I was joking. Half of them said they felt the same way. I can't blame them for not knowing how serious I was. I've said it a few times before. I meant it back then too. Then I'd change my mind and drag myself back there. I knew this time was different but I didn't feel the need to give them any clarification.

That's how my time at Luke ended. I clocked out and walked away. The next day my alarm went off and I ignored it. They called me a few times. I didn't answer. Since I quit in the middle of July my electric bill took a huge jump.

Normally I'd pay twenty to thirty dollars a month for electricity. With me being home more and my air conditioner on full blast all day I ended paying over sixty dollars that month. I feel like there might be at least a few people reading this who scoff at the fact that I'm making a big fuss over a sixty-dollar electric bill but I had no idea when I'd get my next paycheck.

Some of you might wonder how I felt so comfortable making the decision to just stop showing up for work. I did mention earlier that I had planned on quitting. Between my job, grants and my scholarships I had earned approximately $45,000 over the past two years.

I had a little more than $15,000 left in my bank account. This means that I've spent approximately $30,000 over the past two years. So without changing my living habits at all I could live for an entire year on what's in my bank account.

Knowing that it would be a long time before any money went into my account, I decided to make drastic cutbacks on my spending. For the next year of my life I spent less than $800 a month.

I paid $469 a month for rent. The water bill, electric bill and renter's insurance each cost around twenty dollars a month. I switched my cell phone service from Verizon to Ting. The majority of my bills were twenty-five dollars or less. When you add my cable and internet bill, I was spending a bare minimum of $730 per month.

CHAPTER 28

Internship

In my final semester of college, I only had three courses. There were more I was supposed to take but not all the classes on my degree plan were available. My advisor substituted some of the classes I had already taken to count towards my degree plan. I took a Federal Government class and Intro to Humanities. The only class that really mattered was Cooperative Education.

You're only allowed to enroll in the Co-op class if you're planning to graduate at the end of the semester. I signed up thinking they would get me an internship. I showed up to class and the most Mr. O would do is point out places I could apply for.

Most of the people in class were music business students and had much easier times finding jobs. After three weeks with no progress Mr. O made a phone call. I went to interview at InTV, an educational television station that operated out of the school.

I wanted to at least look like I was making an attempt so I wore a polo shirt and a belt. I was interviewed by the woman who owns the station and Jason, the man I'd be working directly under. I was a bit nervous that if the interview didn't go well, I would end up failing the class because I couldn't find the internship. Thankfully they were very welcoming. The interview was just a long conversation where I talked about my goals in life and the things that inspired me to choose this career path.

My Co-op class required me to work fifteen hours a week. Since I had nothing to do on Tuesdays and Thursdays, we decided I could just work those days. My first Tuesday on the job I was there from nine to five. I barely made it out alive.

I'm used to physical stress but this job was mentally exhausting. I talked to Jason and decided I would just work a few hours every afternoon. On days when I had classes I went to the station as soon as my last class ended. Other days I would usually show up around one o'clock.

My favorite thing about this job was saving money on food. I couldn't steal leftovers from the restaurant any more so I had to find some way to save money. There was always sandwich ingredients in the fridge. Once a month they got boxes of food from a food pantry. A lot of it was vegetables so I ate more salads than usual. Plenty of frozen soups. There were also random snacks in there every now and then.

Most of the daily duties involved sitting in front of a computer editing different projects. The hardest part was learning Adobe Suites. Everything I'd been taught was on Avid. All my teachers kept telling us that's what everybody used. They were proven wrong on my very first job.

It was fun playing with Photoshop. I learned a new tool called puppet warp and used it to animate stick figures. It was way too much work and I never want to do it again. Shout out to professional animators everywhere. Your job is difficult.

Anytime I left the office it was usually to film something. Most often filming student concerts on campus. One notable exception was an event known as Sactacular. On a Friday night in October the school courtyard was lined with booths. I wasn't given any specific instructions. Jason just handed me a camera and told me to point it at anything interesting. I spent five hours filming everything in sight as I wandered around aimlessly.

The thing that stood out most about the internship was the insane amount of meetings. Every single one of them dragged on forever. The first day I worked there Jason and Bruce spent an hour discussing the right way to word an email they were sending to NASA requesting more footage. I once followed Jason into a meeting with the owner. That meeting lasted for five hours. I couldn't tell you any of the things they discussed. I was too busy trying to stay wake to pay any attention. At one point in time I was forced to sit through a two-hour lecture about font.

The last lecture I received was on my final day there. Even after my internship ended, I showed up a few more times because I wanted to wrap up a few of my projects. I asked Jason for an opinion on a video I was editing. Jason told me it showed how much knowledge I had gained that I could notice something like that. I made a remark that it wasn't really my knowledge. I only stopped to think "what would Bruce say?" I can't recall their exact words but they managed to correct my thinking.

In the blink of an eye my time at InTV concluded. On my way out the door Jason asked me what my plans were. I had no clue. It's hard to find jobs in media. San Antonio isn't exactly Hollywood. He showed me a few different websites where you can find different jobs throughout town.

He also told me that if I was interested, he had a friend he could call. I show up and work for free and after I've proven myself it could turn into a real job. I said no because half a year had already passed and my bank account kept shrinking. If I had known how difficult it would be to find a job on my own, I would've taken him up on his offer.

CHAPTER 29

Unemployed

I struggled to find work. I applied for many of them but never got responses. There were times when I spent hours on end day after day applying for everything I even slightly qualified for. Other times I'd go an entire month where I didn't bother looking for a job at all.

For the next six months while I was in the middle of this struggle I was thinking about my dreams. With each passing year I grew more disillusioned with Hollywood. Underneath the glitz and glam there's a sleazy underbelly where money is everything.

I was wondering if it was really worth the effort. My college experience was tough enough. I don't want to spend the rest of my life constantly going through the same bull I had to deal with in my production classes.

I'd like to believe that once I get to the top level I'd only be working with the best of the best but there's no guarantee I'd be able to go my entire career without being forced to work with some entitled douche that only got the job because his rich father demanded it.

Most of all I don't want to spend the next thirty years of my life writing someone else's stories. I don't want to spend the next thirty years editing someone else's movies. I can't stand the thought of spending the next thirty years taking orders from idiots on the hope that someday I'll save enough money and build up enough of a reputation that I can finally start working on my own projects. That's why I decided to take matters into my own hands and make a web series.

I knew that the first thing I needed to do was find some help. There was no way I could make this happen on my own. I started thinking of the different people I met in college. The majority of them sucked and I never wanted to see them again. The few of them that might be helpful didn't seem like they'd be worth the trouble.

There was one guy who is very talented and has real world experience. Unfortunately, he's lazy and homophobic and I don't want to be stuck with a guy like that. There's another incredible guy who was far too domineering. I didn't want to work for him. I wanted someone who could work for me.

I narrowed it down to Jeff. We worked so well together in audio production. I contacted him on Facebook with my idea and he was intrigued. We met at the school to discuss how we could make it happen. The first step was to discuss all the different stories we could make.

Jeff had a few good ideas but never got around to writing any of it down. Meanwhile, I wrote three different scripts. One of them was an idea that Josh came up with. One of them was Fire & Ice which I adjusted into a web series. The final one was a brand-new story I created based on some of the experiences I've had with multiple women I've met in my life.

After months of working on these stories, making one edit after another, Jeff came to me with a proposal. He said he'd met a director and producer and told them about our story. They were interested in learning more so Jeff was able to convince me to let him send a few sample scripts. We decided to pause everything while waiting for them to get back to us. They never did. Jeff and I never got back in touch with each other.

As all these other things were going on in my life, I also attempted something new. I was turning twenty-five in a few months and still hadn't been on a single date. I decided to give online dating a chance. I looked at multiple different websites before settling on OkCupid.

It was the only dating website I could find where you actually had the chance to fully immerse yourself without paying a monthly fee. Over the years I've tried multiple websites where I end up paying a fee only to find out their full complement of the features is only one third of the features that OkCupid allows you to access for free.

To this day I still keep a profile on OkCupid. I'm less and less active with every year that passes. When I first signed up, I would be there for hours on end every single day. Nowadays I'll check it a few times a year when I get lonely. The problem with online dating is that a loser in real life can still be a loser on the internet as well.

I've only had five occasions where a woman and I exchanged more than ten messages. With three of them we reached a point where we gave each other our phone numbers and started texting each other, even calling and video chatting a few times. For one reason or another things always fall apart in the end.

When summer approached, I grew nervous. The first month after I quit my job my electric bill doubled from letting the air conditioner run all day. My bank account was continuing to shrink so I decided to go the entire summer without turning the air conditioner on. Over three months of one hundred-degree temperatures. I got a rash twice.

I was existing on nothing but noodles. I'm not talking about ramen. A dollar can get you one cup of ramen or a package of angel hair pasta which can be stretched out over a few meals. So that's all I ate. Plain angel hair pasta. Some days I'd decide to be a little naughty and use butter, salt and pepper. Every now and then I'd even have more than one bowl a day.

After an entire year without a paycheck I reached the point where I could no longer be picky. My bank account was running low. I even started applying to places like McDonald's, Jack in the Box and Bill Miller's. None of them would hire me. Being an adult is hard. September arrived and I had just under three thousand dollars left in my bank accounts. If I continued living on the absolute bare minimum, I could stretch this another five months at most.

Then I logged into Facebook and saw a new message from Crystal asking me if I was looking for a job. I said yes. She told me that the restaurant she currently worked at was in desperate need of a dishwasher. She recommended me. All I had to do was show up at this address at four o'clock Tuesday afternoon and start working. I find it funny to look back on my life. I've only had three paying jobs. All of them were dishwasher. All of them were given to me because I knew somebody.

Everything Is Impossible

CHAPTER 30

Gwendolyn

I was starting a new job at a restaurant called Gwendolyn. It's a little hole in the wall that the average person has probably never heard of. The majority of their clientele are there for business dinners and anniversaries. Some of them are just Foodies or tourists.

They have a dress code for customers. Business causal or better. I was worried they might take one look and decide I don't fit. I trimmed my beard to make sure it was even. I'd been keeping my hair short. I made sure to comb it and my beard hair before I left the apartment. I put on my favorite polo and wore a belt.

I left my apartment around three in the afternoon. Since I didn't recognize the address, I didn't want to risk being late on my first day. I arrived there around 3:30 and walked in the door nervous and unsure. I was greeted by a skinny white man resembling Mr. Clean. That man was Chef Mike. He walked me around the restaurant showing me how to clean the restrooms and the windows then sweep and mop the dining room floor. Then we went downstairs and started scrubbing pots and pans.

The mission statement of the restaurant was to get back to the core of cooking. Chef Mike was tired of how corporate the industry had become. Everything at Gwendolyn was done the old-fashioned way. No technology at all. Everything made by hand from scratch. They get an entire pig delivered to them and they chop it up using saws, knives and hand cranked grinders.

This also means that I don't have a machine. Every single plate, pan and pot has to be washed by hands. Despite that the most difficult thing about this job is the spiral staircase. Not even joking when I say it gives you vertigo.

In my early days at Gwen people kept finding different reasons to yell at me. Every single day someone would tell me something I wasn't doing well enough or something I wasn't told I was supposed to be doing. To be fair, half of the things they told me were my responsibility were not my responsibility.

My first clue should've been the fact that when Chef Mike trained me, he never told me to do the welcome mats. When the front of the house manager complained that the dishwasher before usually did them Chef took her side. Then I noticed a recurring pattern.

Every time a new server started working there, they would clean the mats and put them out. They had to be told not to do it because it's Nathan's job. The reason that every new server thought it was their job is because it was on the server's list of responsibilities. Not mine.

I had worked there for three months when Chef walked up to me while I was sweeping the floor and told me I was doing everything wrong. He said there was no way to finish the floor because it takes half an hour to mop it properly. That's a lie. I've got it down to fifteen minutes. The point is I've been there three months before you finally decided to tell me that; everything I do has a time limit. That would've been great information to tell me on my first day.

I'm not actively planning to leave that job any time soon but when I do go, I'm going to present my replacement with a fully typed ten-page training manual with all the information that Chef neglected to tell me. If he ever tries to claim that he taught me everything I know he's a liar. He taught me the bare basics. Nearly ninety percent of what I know about my hob I had to figure out as I went.

I cried that day. Chef Mike was standing in front of me telling me that I'd need to be trained from square one. If someone has been there for three months and still doesn't understand how to do their job it means one of two things: Either they're a complete idiot and they're never going to understand or you never explained their job properly. It made me feel horrible to hear someone tell me I wasn't doing well enough.

It took another three months before I finally felt comfortable. I'm just a dishwasher. Physically my job is the toughest in the building. Anyone who wants to disagree can feel free to take my place for a day. Tell me how you feel after spending six straight hours going up and down a spiral staircase every five minutes carrying a bus tub with twenty pounds worth of dishes.

That being said, there's a reason I've stayed at dishwasher all these years. Chef keeps trying to convince me to be a cook and I keep telling him no. There are two good things about being a dishwasher. Number one is the autonomy. Now that I've earned their trust, they leave me alone. As long as the dishes get clean, they have no reason to ever say anything to me. Number two is that the job is only physically demanding.

Once I found my rhythm, I reached a point where most days I can operate on autopilot and still impress them. Some days I spend my entire shift writing a new song or workshopping different story ideas. Recently I've spent half my shifts working on this autobiography.

That's the main reason I refuse to go to the kitchen. It actually requires the use of your brain. There's no such thing as comfortable in that kitchen. Not when you have a boss that could give you a three-hour lecture covering the unabridged history of the rice grain.

If I had to give you an oversimplified description of Chef Mike, I would describe him as an idiot savant. There have been three separate occasions when he said something so stupid that I wondered how he actually managed to survive this long in life. He's not impossibly dumb. Just below average.

If a normal human has an IQ of one hundred then Chef's is probably in the mid-eighties. Capable of deeper understand but only through great effort. Luckily for him he's a natural scholar and has picked up many skills along the way. As an everyday man he's as close to average as anyone can be. Then he steps into the kitchen and transforms into a genius. I'm not joking when I tell you this man could tell you the entire history of the rice grain.

Meeting him taught me a lot. I found it fascinating that any human being could know that much about food. The history of it as well as the scientific aspects. I realized I'm that way myself. I know way more about movies, music and everything pop culture than the majority of people I've interacted with in my life. It's not like I was born with all that knowledge in my head. I looked it up because I wanted to know more. I retained the knowledge because the answers I found fascinated me.

When you read this book there might be times when you find yourself wondering why I'm able to recall certain details of my five-year-old thought process when I can't tell you the names of half the people, I see at work every day. The only thing I can say is that we humans all seem to have a special little quirk in common. People in general seem to have an easier time remembering something when they actually care about it. So if your husband never remembers your anniversary then you should definitely divorce him.

If I had to pick the one thing, I hate most about Chef Mike it is definitely that he's far too trusting. He chooses to believe in people. He once told me something that I found hilarious. I believe his exact words were "I truly believe that if you clearly lay out the difference between right and wrong, this is right, this is wrong, this is why, that no one will come to work and choose to do the wrong thing." It took every ounce of strength in my body not to laugh in his face. Have you ever met any human being ever? There are far too many horrible people on this planet for you to be this naïve.

There's a person in the building who proves Chef wrong on a daily basis. Not even daily. He proves Chef wrong every five minutes. His name is Julio. Throughout this book I've gone out of my way not to mention the people I've hated. Most of the time this was easy because the things they did to me meant more than the person that did them. Julio is an exception.

I've been made aware that everyone at Kimura thinks I hate them. I don't hate any of them. I only hate Julio. I barely pay attention to any of the others. There are around thirty people working there and I can only name four of them.

Julio used to work at Gwen. He said he was leaving because they wouldn't give him enough hours. The sous chef said that Julio told them he could only work on Wednesdays. My second day on the job was his final day. There were very obvious things that he was doing wrong. Half of it was just him being lazy, I didn't say anything to him because I knew he'd be gone tomorrow and I'd never have to deal with him again. I was very wrong.

I just realized I haven't told you about Kimura yet. It is a Japanese restaurant owned by the same company that owns Gwendolyn. We share the same building. They have a bad habit of borrowing things from us. They'll often come over to grab something of ours without telling anyone and with no intention of ever bringing it back. I'm fairly certain that if you look up the word borrow in the dictionary that is the exact definition.

This was a huge point of contention between me and Julio. Every time someone at Kimura broke their deck brush or squeegee, Julio would come over to Gwen and grab ours. He would grab our good one saying "this is ours" and leave the broken one for us. Then we'd buy a new one. A few weeks later Kimura would break theirs again and Julio would stomp back over. He'd hold up the broken one saying "this is yours" then grab the good one and storm out of the room saying "this is ours."

I spent the first year and a half complaining about every single thing that Julio did in a desperate effort to get him fired. I figured if I complained enough, they would eventually get tired of hearing it and they'd get rid of one of us. That never happened. I overheard a conversation where one of my coworkers asked a manager why they don't fire Julio. That manager said "they won't fire him because…"

I didn't hear that part of the conversation. I only picked up a small portion of it as I was walking past. The answer didn't matter. I don't need to know the specific reason. Now

I know that every single person who has worked with Julio hates him and the only reason they don't fire him is because they aren't allowed to. It put my mind at ease. I worked with Julio for two and a half years and never heard anybody say a single good thing about him.

CHAPTER 31

2016

Once I settled in at Gwendolyn I decided to contact Jeff. I wanted to take another shot at making web shows. Things went slightly better this time. We rewrote the scripts to better accommodate our budget. Fire & Ice was rewritten to entirely take place in one apartment. Jeff also brought in a friend of his to help us improve our stories. We even began finding actors. We still struggled through some issues.

We kept finding different things to argue about. Our partnership ended on the dumbest possible fight. We were trying to schedule a meeting and couldn't agree on the medium. He kept demanding that we use skype and I kept asking what was wrong with a phone call. I guess he felt my question didn't dignify an answer. Every time I asked, he refused to respond. I probably would've caved eventually if he had just given me a reason.

I don't blame Jeff for things a falling apart. I don't think either of us handled the situation as well as we could have. We weren't experienced enough, capable enough or motivated enough to bring an ambitious idea like this to life. I was trying to rely on him to handle everything hoping that

I could just stand in the background shouting orders. Once again, an attempt to chase my dreams falls short.

After that I decided to just enjoy my life for a while. I started at ten dollars an hour at Gwen. After the first year I moved up to eleven dollars an hour. At Luke I earned twelve hundred dollars on my best month ever. That was the time I worked a double and ended up with nearly sixty hours in one week.

Working at Gwen I'd have slow weeks where I'm working six to eight hours a day and sometimes getting days off. I'm still getting fourteen hundred dollars even on those months. I've gotten as much as eighteen hundred dollars on some really busy months.

I'm so used to living far below my means and now I'm making more money than I know how to spend. My cable bill jumped over two hundred dollars and I didn't care. I got a new cell phone when I started at Gwen. A year later the next generation came out and I bought it just because I could. No matter how much money I spent I always had more.

Both my bank accounts kept growing. I could order pizza or grab some fast food any time I want without a care because my job required so much of me physically that I didn't have to worry about getting fat. This is the best shape I've been I've ever been in.

Yet, with all the things going right, I was unhappy. It wasn't just the depression talking. There are definitely times when I can't make it through a day without crying but that's not what I'm talking about right now. On an entirely different level I felt completely unfulfilled.

This led to me investing way too much energy into my job. I cared way too much about everything that happened in that building. I had nothing else to focus my passion on. Doing well at work was the only goal I could set for myself. It drove me crazy.

A few people have told me not to omit this next section from the book entirely but it's a key factor in the story because of the mental effect it had on me. In the summer of 2016 Christina Grimmie was murdered. I didn't want to believe it when I first heard the news. It took about three months to fully come to terms with the fact that she was gone. I spent hours on end listening to Hear You Me by Jimmy Eat World on repeat.

I could never have guessed that it would've affected me so much. Plenty of celebrities have died before. I've spent my entire life loving Robin Williams and Whitney Houston and didn't shed a single tear when they died. I grew to realize that I was so shocked by Christina's death because it's the first time that a celebrity younger than me died. I know that Selena, Tupac and Biggie were all murdered in their early twenties but I was only five and six years old.

Christina Grimmie was four years younger than me and had already accomplished so much. Meanwhile I'm still washing dishes for a living. So many talented people keep being taken from this world. Why am I still here? No one needs me. Their lives were so much more impactful. They've done more good than I ever could. If someone told me that my death could bring any of them back, I wouldn't hesitate to make the sacrifice. If my presence was completely erased from existence nothing about this world would change.

Before you read the second half of this chapter would you mind doing me a favor my dear reader? Take a second to stop and think…when's the last time I mentioned any of my relatives? What was the last chapter where I talked about my mother, sister or uncle? The last time I saw my uncle was during my internship.

Since my sister finished high school, I'll see her only on holidays, if at all. I visit my grandmother once every few months. My mother even less than that. I jumped at the opportunity to go to a friend's house for thanksgiving because it meant I could avoid my relatives.

A few days before Christmas my sister, uncle and I received a group text from my mom saying that my grandmother was in the hospital. I was at work when I got the text. My grandmother fell in the bathroom. She didn't slip or anything like that. She simply fell. Her legs just stopped working and she went to the ground.

My grandmother is a stubborn woman and told my mom to just not touch her. She spent the entire night lying on the bathroom floor. When she woke the next morning and still couldn't move, she allowed my mom to call an ambulance. I spent that Christmas alone in my apartment watching TV.

I couldn't tell you the specific details of what was wrong with her. All I know for sure is that she had to have surgery and was in the hospital for over a month. I kept promising I would visit but had no intention of actually doing so. I was trying my best not to think about it.

A small part of me knew I had no reason to worry. That stubborn old witch will outlive us all and dance on our graves. Then again, she's in her seventies. There are so many things that can go wrong with any surgery.

Something struck me. For the life of me I could not understand why I cared so much. I hate all my relatives. Her more than anyone. She caused me so much pain. She's made me shed more blood and tears than any other human on this planet. If I ever snap and kill someone, I guarantee you I will blame her. Everything wrong in my life is her fault. So why does the thought of her dying scare me so much.

It took me a while to figure it out the reason for my mixed emotions. This was the woman who raised me. I've never known a world where she didn't exist. She taught me to cook. She taught me to clean, which is every paying job I've ever had. She taught me a great work ethic and unfortunately taught me how to deal with difficult and utterly unreasonable people. I was more self-sufficient at age ten than some forty-year-olds I've met. Most of all I've never questioned whether or not she'd be there for me.

I spent much of my adult life telling people I never had a mother. I use the word mother in this book so there's no confusion as to who I'm referencing. In private conversations I often refer to her as the woman who gave birth to me. Some people would say I should be grateful to her for giving me the gift of life. Well, I've spent more than half my life wishing I was never born so I don't believe I have anything to thank her for.

I spent most of my childhood scoffing at every movie and TV show where the kid turns out exactly like their parent. It didn't feel realistic. A generic and overused plot device. I actively chose the person I wanted to become in an effort to avoid being anything like my relatives. Turns out I've got a lot in common with the woman who raised me.

I got her loyalty and dedication. She taught me her work ethic. Just like her I'm mistakenly thought to be fiercely independent when really, I'm just incredibly selective about the company I keep. We both get lonely. More important than anything else... I got her stubbornness.

For better or worse, I would not be the person I am today if she hadn't been part of my life. She's the biggest factor in me becoming who I am today. She made me kind. She made me angry. She made me compassionate. She made it hard for me to trust. She made me loyal. She made me stubborn.

She made me Nathan. Yet here I am feeling a sense of relief at the thought of her dying. I've never stopped feeling guilty about that. She may have raised me wrong... but at least she tried. That's more than you can say about a lot of parents.

> "The plan is to show you that I understand.
> You are appreciated."
>
> – Tupac Shakur. *Dear Mama.*

CHAPTER 32

Brenda

This chapter will focus entirely on my interaction with a woman named Brenda who I met at work. Before she worked there her position was held by a guy named Reyes. Of all the employees that ever worked at Gwendolyn he's my absolute favorite. When you include every coworker from every job, I've ever had he's still top four. When Reyes left, I promised him I'd hate whoever replaced him.

The restaurant was closed for the first week of January. When we returned to work Brenda was there. Our friendship began that very first day. While we were in the middle of closing duties, she asked me what my favorite anime was. Apparently, she overheard me having a conversation with Chef Mike earlier in the day asking him about some food I'd seen on a show I watched that morning. I wanted to keep my promise to Reyes but I also love talking about my favorite anime.

From day one there where things I hated about Brenda. She was overly confrontational. The first argument we ever had was over a Disney cartoon. We were having a conversation and I mentioned in passing that The Hunchback of Notre

Dame was my favorite Disney cartoon because it was the most realistic. She responded by angrily shouting "how dare you say Beauty and the Beast isn't realistic!" Just because I said something was more realistic doesn't mean I'm deeming everything else in the world completely beyond belief. I can say I enjoy nachos more without it automatically meaning I hate pizza.

I learned early on that it's best to always have multiple topics prepared anytime I speak to Brenda. If I ever felt she was gearing up to fight I could quickly change to a less disputable subject. She grew so accustomed to me erratically jumping from one subject to another that she accepted it as one of my quirks. The fact that regularly switching between unrelated topics became so common shows just how often I felt like she was being confrontational.

I don't like arguing. It's something I prefer to do only out of necessity. There are moments when I feel that someone's way of thinking desperately needs to be corrected. The rest of the time I just don't care. Especially when it concerns trivial subjects like a person's favorite song or movie. There's simply no accounting for taste. You explaining why you like your favorite movie more than you like my favorite movie isn't going to magically make me like my favorite movie any less.

As troubling as her constant desire for discourse was there was one thing Brenda did that bothered me far more. She was always late. The earliest she's ever shown up was fifteen minutes late. There was one occasion when she arrived six hours late. She said she wanted to spend time with me but had a lot of errands to run. She asked if she could pick me up early, around ten in the morning, and we could spend the day together while I helped her run errands. At ten o'clock I was showered and dressed. After waiting two hours with no response I texted her asking when she'd be come. She said she'd come get me after she was done running her errands.

Brenda has a hard time remembering facts. Her brain somehow manages to generate whatever memories are necessary for her to be correct. There's that time she invited me to her birthday party. When I said I couldn't go she "reminded" me that the party was next week. I was looking at the message she sent. She didn't say next Monday. Didn't give any specific date. Her text only said Monday. Most people would probably assume that you meant the upcoming Monday.

In that same conversation she told me that she would pick me up early next week and I could help her set up the party. The day of the party I kept waiting for her to show up and she never did. I called to ask her when she'd show up. Can you guess what she said? "I can't pick you up right now. I'm too busy setting up the party."

Brenda has trouble with details. I've seen many people struggle with this. Chef Mike does it all the time. I do it as well. I don't think it would be too much of a stretch to guess that you've done it yourself reader. You say something that makes total sense to you. Then you're shocked when the person you're talking to doesn't understand what you meant.

Well, at least I can admit when I'm wrong. Brenda is one of those people that never has to apologize because she's never been wrong in her life.

Despite all the negative things I've said about Brenda I generally enjoyed spending time with her. It was too much work but most of the time it was fun. Unfortunately, every friendship goes through some turbulent times. We've had a few fights. This one was different. I remember every single word each of us said. You only need to know the last sentence Brenda said. Those words still piss me off. "I've heard your sob story so many times that it means nothing to me. Everybody has a hard life."

Let's dissect this argument piece by piece. To start with, this isn't a sob story – you imperious louse. This is my life. You're tired of hearing it? You've known me a year. You've heard me mention my childhood traumas three times. I've relived those events over and over in my head millions of times. It never stops hurting. I am who I am because of the life I've lived. If my past means nothing to you then I mean nothing to you.

Everybody has a hard life. That's her catch phrase. She says it anytime I try to complain about anything. Hashtag first world problems. People say these things as if it's supposed to make you feel better. It always makes me feel worse. Why does everyone on this planet keep telling me that I'm not allowed to feel pain?

Everybody has a bad life? Sure. Everyone on this planet has relatives who beat them till they bled. Everyone on this planet has spent their entire life lying to every single person they meet about their sexual history because they're too ashamed to admit that they were raped as a child. Everyone on this planet has hated their lives and themselves so much that they tried to kill themselves multiple times.

Everyone has a hard life. The fact that you feel comfortable saying something like that proves to me that you've had it pretty easy. I was watching an episode of Reba where she met Santa Claus. He told her something that I think everyone on this planet needs to understand. "There's always someone suffering worse than you. That doesn't mean your pain doesn't count."

I don't hate Brenda. There are times when I still wish I could hang out with her. She's not evil. She's just not a good fit for me. I've heard it said many times before, mostly about sports, that rather than getting the most talented person you need to find the person that best fits your needs. I think that applies to all interpersonal relationships.

Brenda has a good heart. She just doesn't understand my heart. She never tried to understand. She didn't take the time to get to know me. She learned a few things about me and filled in the rest on her own. After knowing me for only one year she sincerely seemed to believe that she knew more about me than I did.

It became apparent that she didn't really know me as Nathan. I was placed in the same category as every other human being in the world with a penis. I can't say I'm any better. I had trouble seeing Brenda as a human being. I treated her more like an imaginary friend. I thought we had everything in common because we had so many similar interests. I was wrong. Other than loving the same things we had nothing in common.

CHAPTER 33

The Beginning

So this is it. The final chapter. I wasn't sure if writing this book would be worth the effort. I've always thought my life was boring. I never learned to ride a bike. Never learned to swim. I've never sat behind the wheel of a car. Never been arrested. Still haven't been on a date. Every woman who has seen my penis is a doctor or a relative.

The good news is I've never lost a game of never have I ever. Unless the goal is to actually get drunk in which case, I lose every single time. Only recently have I learned that the things that make my life different are what make my life interesting. They say you should only compare apples to apples. If the majority of humans on this planet are apples then I'm a burnt chicken nugget served on a melted marshmallow drizzled with cranberry sauce and uncooked rice sprinkled on top.

Quick rehash of where my life was in the summer of 2017. I had just turned twenty-seven. I haven't been to the optometrist since 2012, the doctor since 2011 and the dentist since 2010. If you're wondering "What about Obamacare?" I was exempt from penalties the first few years because I made so little money. The first year I paid a penalty was 2017 and it amounted to less than one paycheck. Even the cheapest plans could cost twice that much for a full year of coverage. Why pay for something I'm not actually going to use. If I'm just giving money away, I'll choose the cheapest option.

Despite how cheap I normally am I have begun spending recklessly. No matter how carelessly I spend my bank accounts keep growing. I get to stuff my face with ice cream, candy and soda. I eat way too much fast food. Every weekend I get pizza. Not to mention a Taco Bell and Dunkin Donuts recently opening up a few streets away. I currently own a thirty-inch flat screen, two laptops, three tablets, a smartphone and a Bluetooth speaker and headphones. Not to mention spending over two hundred dollars a month on cable and internet.

In high school I took three showers a day and was always caked in deodorant. I could never make it through a single class period without someone telling me how much I stunk. Now I shower four times a week and haven't worn deodorant in six or seven years. No one ever says anything. Did I finally get rid of my B.O. or are high school teens just that mean?

I've gotten better at cleaning my apartment. I'll still only do it three times a year on threat of eviction. So you can only see the floor three weeks out of the year. At least now it only takes me three hours to clean instead of an entire week.

For some reason the apartment managers decided to start opening the fridge door to check inside and make sure it's clean. This feels like an invasion of privacy but I'm glad they did it. By forcing me to clean my fridge I actually learned how it worked. Now that my fridge is fully operational, I can start buying things like lunch meat, cheese, fruit juice and yogurt.

Working at Gwendolyn has aged me physically. My bones and muscles ache often. Then again, this is the best shape I've ever been in. On a busy day I'll walk up and down that spiral staircase fifty times. Each time carrying at least twenty pounds worth of dishes. Do you know how often I have to squat down to grab a heavy load and rise straight up? It's not easy. I may have a big belly but there is less than one percent body fat below my waist

As I'm writing this rough draft, I weigh 270 pounds. My weight has risen as high as 290 pounds. Nearly 300 pounds and I can still squeeze into size thirty-eight pants. You tiny people might be thinking that thirty eight is huge but that is the smallest my waistline is capable of getting. I'm touching my waist right now and I feel bone.

I'm a wide man. Wide shoulders, wide feet, wide child bearing hips. My body was meant to carry a lot of weight. A former coworker once commented, "People with bodies like ours are the reasons Africans made such great slaves."

Despite the physical toll on my body there's a reason I've stayed at the job this long. The job is physically demanding but at least my mind is free. There are times when I spend the entire night working on a song or writing a new movie.

If anyone at work has ever seen me with my phone out in the middle of a shift allow me to blow your minds. I rarely ever text anyone. I'm never on the internet. If you see my phone in my hand, I'm usually writing song lyrics. Sometimes I'm in the middle of a story and feel like I need to keep writing or risk losing my mojo. Fun fact: I wrote three chapters of this book at work. I wrote the first half of this chapter at a bus stop.

Chef Mike has tried many times to convince me to be a cook. I keep telling him no. Do you remember me telling you how he knows the entire history of the rice grain? If you ask him whether or not you should squirt lemon juice on something, he'll give you an hour-long lecture about the complete unabridged history of the lemon.

Every now and then he'll give his cooks a test. From what I understand his tests are a single question. When you give the wrong answer, he gives you a two-hour lecture explaining all the reasons why you were wrong. If I work in the kitchen, I'll actually have to take my job home. I'll never love food that much.

Julio's still there. He's not as stupid as everyone says. He's also not as lazy. There are times when he'll go out of his way to do something wrong when it would've been much easier to do his job correctly. There was a point when he started leaving a huge mess for me every morning.

Every single day I'd show up to work and there'd either be a trash can full of sludge or a sink full of bones. When I kept complaining about this, he changed his game. I showed up to work and the grate that covered the sink was gone. I had to dig bones out of the drain.

If it happened once then maybe you could've said it was an accident. It happened eighteen times. I know for a fact that it's Julio but I get in trouble if I accuse him without proof. All my evidence is circumstantial. The only thing that all eighteen of those disappearances have in common is that Julio was in the room. There are only four times that it happened when I was at work. All four times Julio was the only one in the room. I'd drain the sinks then clean and refill them. All three grates were in place. I'd take clean dishes upstairs.

When I was coming back downstairs with dirty dishes, I'd see Julio either at the sink or leaving the room. Then I look in the sink and one of the grates is gone. There were three other times when I walked back downstairs as he was walking to the sink and managed to catch him with a grate in his hand. When he saw me, he pretended he was dumping out some food and put the grate back in place.

I went to family dollar and found some mesh grates that cost a dollar each. I bought thirty of them. I need grates in those sinks. Pure and simple. If too much food goes down the drain it'll eventually clog. Then I'll have to shut down the sink, no matter how busy the restaurant might be that day, and tear all the pipes apart trying to find the clog and clear it. Spending some money to make sure I always have grates available is the much easier option.

I stopped complaining about Julio. I'm not worried about getting him fired anymore. Instead of trying to stop him from doing stupid things my main focus has become making sure that I always have the things I need to fulfill my job duties. If I use it on a daily basis, I've got a backup of it hidden somewhere in the building. I needed a permanent solution. Since murdering Julio is out of the question the only thing I can do is have a plan prepared so I'm never caught off-guard by the dumb things he does.

Update: a month after finishing the rough draft Julio quit. More than fifty percent of the things that went wrong on a daily basis stopped immediately the day he left. The negative things that did continue happened far less frequently.

There are two explanations for why they continued at all. One reason is that some of these things were institutional. Everyone who ever has or ever will work there will continue doing it. Reason two is part of the reason why things have become institutional. For some reason they actually let Julio train a lot of the newbies. He spent years teaching new employees the wrong ways to do their jobs.

I was struggling through a severe depressive bought. There was a three-month period where I was feeling more suicidal than usual. Any time I left my apartment I thought about closing my eyes and walking into traffic. With my luck I would only break every bone in my body and severely damage many of my internal organs. Unfortunately, I'd still be alive. I'd empty my bank accounts paying the hospital bills and lose my job because my body can't handle the demands.

I reached a point where I felt like I had no choice but to give up. Not just on my dreams but on life in general. I'm a twenty-seven-year-old man who's never been on a date and is living alone in a one room apartment washing dishes for a living. It's impossible not to be depressed when I look at the world around me and it seems like every single human being on the planet is living a much happier life than I am. I've lost count of how many times I've cried myself to sleep. I've lost count of how many times I've woken up disappointed because I realized this isn't a horrible nightmare. This really is my life. I'm still stuck here.

> **"They should've shot me when I was born. Now I'm trapped in the mother fucking storm."**
> – Tupac Shakur. *How Long Will They Mourn Me.*

I knew I needed to make some changes but wasn't sure where to start. I looked up foster care in San Antonio. I considered signing up to be a child advocate. I decided it wasn't right for me to take responsibility for someone else when I can't even get my own life together.

I visited a tattoo parlor and talked to an employee. We spent about half an hour discussing designs, prices and time frames. I legitimately considered emptying my bank account to cover my entire body, from the shoulders down, in tattoos. I might've gone through with it if not for Nina.

Nina was a woman who worked at Kimura. A few years younger than me. A few inches taller. Her hair has had some different colors but most of the time it was blonde. She'd been there basically the entire time I worked at

Gwen. I didn't pay much attention to her that first year. She was some random face that popped into view every now and them.

Then came that summer day, somewhere in July of 2016, when I went to throw some trash in the dumpster. Kimura's door was open. Nina was standing just inside the doorway. I noticed her mouth was moving. I looked down and saw a half-eaten apple in her hand. When I looked back at her face, she started chewing with her mouth open. In that moment I knew I needed someone like her in my life. Six months later I said hi to her.

For the first few months are interactions were minimal. Every now and then we'd cross each other's paths and say hi. Our longest conversations lasted three sentences. Despite the lack of exposure, I found myself falling for her. The more I talked to her the more I wanted to talk to her. One day I asked for her phone number and her response was "I actually have a boyfriend, but..."

She held onto that final word for about three seconds. It was the longest pause of my life. What are you planning to say? Was she going to tell me that she has a boyfriend but she's polyamorous and wouldn't mind adding me to her list of lovers? Was she about to say that her boyfriend is something new and it's not that serious yet? That she wouldn't mind having a secret fling with me? Say something woman!

The silence was killing me so I interrupted her pause with a preplanned response. There's a reason I asked for her phone number instead of asking her on a date or asking if she was single. It was an escape plan. This way if she turned me down in any way, I could say it wasn't meant in a romantic way.

I told her that she seemed interesting and I wanted to be able to talk to her more. We're never in the same room together for more than twenty seconds. She gave me here number and we started texting. Over the months we got closer. Then she stopped working at Kimura and we slowly started to lose contact.

The reason I mention Nina isn't because I was depressed about things not working out again. I've come to expect that. I mention Nina is because she inspired me to write three songs about her. Those songs were call One Chance (Tonight), About Me and Show Me Your World. About Me is the most important of those three. It's the first time I've written a song for Amanda's Little Brother since I finished high school.

When I wrote About Me it rekindled a long-extinguished spark. I had written five songs since leaving Haven. Now suddenly I've written three in one month. I'd forgotten how therapeutic songwriting can be. I kept writing more. Since I was writing new music for Amanda's Little Brother, I decided to look at all the old music. I ended up rewriting half the songs. It has been ten years after all. My abilities have improved since then.

Since I was rewriting the songs, I decided to take a stab at rewriting the story. Half of the songs from season two were put into season one. Most of the new songs I wrote were put in season two. A few were put in seasons four and five. I changed many major details including renaming the show Amanda's Little Brother.

When I rewrote season one, I transformed it from an hour-long television drama with twelve episodes into a ten-minute web series with twenty-two episodes. That's when it struck me. I wasn't writing this for fun. I wrote it as if I was going to try and make it right now. Dear god I haven't given up on my dreams.

I looked at my bank account. There's $15,000 in there. I wondered if I should contact Jeff and see if he's willing to try again. This time I'm willing to dip into my bank account so we have a budget to pay people. I plan on being a better leader this time around.

Then I thought about how difficult it is to make money that way. After much deliberation I decided I should start with print media. After looking over every single story I've ever written I decided that Toxic is the best story to bring to life. After all, it is my oldest and most fleshed out story.

As I was editing Oscar's storyline to perfection something happened. I was watching YouTube videos when for some reason Anna Kendrick popped up in my suggestions. She was doing some sort of interview for her book Scrappy Little Nobody. It pissed me off.

Why does every celebrity need to write a book about their life? Why does everyone say how inspirational it is? I know my opinion probably doesn't matter to someone who has sold millions of copies with her book but how am I supposed to be inspired by someone who's been getting paid jobs since they were nine?

What reason to I have to believe in myself? What reason do I have to reach for the stars? What reason do I have to hope for a happy life? Logically speaking I know this is all folly. I keep trying because it's the only thing I've ever wanted in life. I'll never be fully satisfied with my life if I don't achieve this goal. I also know I don't want to spend the next twenty years answering the same questions about my childhood over and over again in every single interview. That's why I decided to write my autobiography now.

I thought it would be more meaningful to hear the story of chasing your dreams from the perspective of someone who has yet to achieve them. I'd say I have no reason to believe I'll ever achieve them but it's not one hundred percent correct. I made the decision to start writing this book in July 2017. I finished the rough draft in March 2018. I finished my final draft in May 2019. It's still ninety three percent accurate but I have a few reasons to believe this little venture of mine could actually prove profitable. I can't tell you the details. If I do that now I'll have nothing to write in my next book.

Everything Is Impossible

CHAPTER 34

Clarifications

Before you put this book down forever, I figured I should take some time to clear up a few misconceptions. Let's start with my relatives. I don't hate them. At least, I don't want to. Some days it's hard not to. I'm still holding onto a lot of anger.

I don't want them in my life but after thirty years I've come to just accept the fact that they'll always be there. I feel the same way about them that I do my glasses. I don't like them but there are times when they make my life easier. There are also times when they drive me crazy and wish I'd never had them in the first place.

I don't hate religion. There are many people in my life that I hold a great amount of respect for who are very devout. I don't blame religion for the choices my mother made. I just can't bring myself to worship.

I was raised southern Baptist but my current beliefs are closer to deism and agnosticism. I choose to live an atheist life. Even if someone can prove to me that every single word in the bible is a fact I still won't worship. I'm just not the type of person that can blindly follow a leader. There's a reason I never joined the army.

Since I'm still going to be working at Gwendolyn when this book gets published, I have a message for a few of you. Don't start talking to me right when I walk in the door. I'm not pretending I can't hear you. I turn the volume up on my headphones specifically to drown out people's voices. Don't start talking to me the second I take off my headphones either. I hate talking to people before I have my coffee. I don't drink coffee.

Also, stop calling me Nate. It's the most boring and unoriginal thing you could possibly call me. I've always hated being called Nate. My name is Nathan. If you don't want to call me that then come up with an actual nickname with some sort meaning. I've had many people in my life come up with much better nicknames than Nate. As a teen I was known as Ben Wallace, Chocolate Thunder, Biggie and Bubba. I accept all of those names. What's the story behind Nate? You're just too lazy to say a two-syllable word.

I hate when people call me patient. I have no patience. The definition of patience is that a person can handle stressful situations without getting upset. What I have is self-control. Everything pisses me off. I just don't let it show. I spend most days wanting to punch almost every single human being I see. There are days when I've got far too much anger to contain and I begin taking it out on people who don't deserve it.

Some people seem to think that I'm stuck up because I'm constantly bragging about how smart I am. Firstly, I never brag. I'm simply stating something that I consider to be a verifiable fact. My brain clearly operates on a higher level than the majority of humans I've interacted with in my life. I have to keep reminding myself that everyone else is normal. I'm the freak.

I get easily frustrated when other people can't grasp the simplest concepts. Then I try to explain it to them and realize how complicated it actually is. I keep having to tell myself "just because you understand it doesn't mean it's easy to understand."

I realize that some people might think I'm pompous after reading that last paragraph. If you think I have a high opinion of myself I suggest you read this book again. I don't think I'm better than anyone just because I'm smarter than them. There's no human being I hate more than myself.

While I do value intelligence it is not the sole measure of a person's worth. There are other qualities I consider far more important. Things like kindness, compassion, and empathy. I'd rather spend time with a kind moron than an arrogant genius. I'm sure most people feel that way. That's probably why I don't have any friends.

Throughout my life people have been telling me how shy I am. I've come to learn that all of them were wrong. I'm not shy. I'm an introvert. A shy person craves social interactions and hesitates out of fear. An introvert is more than capable of interacting with others and simply lacks the desire to do so. It's understandable why those two are used synonymously. From the outside a shy person and an introvert might seem identical. The difference is internal.

Due to many negative experiences I've also become a misanthrope. So I don't feel the need for constant social interaction and even when I do I'm incredibly picky about the people I interact with. Throughout the years many people I've worked with ask me why I don't go drinking with them after work. It's because I need a break from you people.

The eight hours a day I spend trapped in this building with you counts as my friend time for the day. I need a few hours to myself to wind down so I don't accidently end up killing one of you on purpose. For those wondering, sleep doesn't count as alone time.

It's true that I'm often hesitant, especially in new places with new people. It's not out of fear. I have a scientific mind. I prefer to observe and learn. I want to have the most complete understanding possible of my surroundings and the people in it.

I've noticed that the hesitance I experience when asking women out has an explanation. I get more and more nervous about asking someone out as I get older. Years of rejection keep piling on top of each other. Now when I like someone my brain just won't shut up. I don't take half year to work up the courage to ask out someone I like. I take half a year to convince myself that it's actually worth making the effort.

Everyone on the planet should know that there's nothing wrong with being alone, if that's what you want. You shouldn't live your life just to fit into other people's opinions of normal. I don't mind being alone. Most of the time I prefer it. I'd rather be alone than to be stuck with the wrong person. Then, every once in a while, there are those nights when the loneliness is so strong that I feel physical pain.

I'm sure there are plenty of psychologist who could critically analyze this book and tell you every logical reason why I want a relationship. I'm not sure it would be the worst thing in the world for me to die alone. I've been alone my entire life. I've gotten used to it by now.

Even if by some miracle a living breathing woman somehow does manage to fall in love with me I can almost one hundred percent guarantee that I'll find some way to screw it up. There's an often-quoted Shakespearean line that, "it is better to have loved and lost than to never have loved at all." The truth is, we'll never know for sure. Whatever you're going through right now you're probably wishing it was the other one.

I've also heard it said that no one else can love you if you don't love yourself. I think I understand what that means. I hate myself. I don't consider myself to be someone worth loving. When anyone else tells me they care about me I don't want to believe that they're being sincere. I know that they believe what they're saying but I can always find a logical explanation why they're wrong.

I've also come to realize that I want to be loved more than I want to love. I don't really have the time or desire for a relationship. I just want to know that someone cares about me so fully and completely. To know that someone is utterly devoted. To know someone will always be there to welcome me home. To know that I'm the most important person in their life. I get it now. I don't need a girlfriend. I need a dog.

I need more people in my life that I can use as a sounding board to vent my frustrations. I spend at least an hour or two every week just pacing around my apartment complaining about every single thing that's going wrong in my life. There are times when my imaginary friends aren't enough to get me through. They're too honest to be of any real comfort.

I need someone to lie to me. I need someone to hug me and tell me it'll be alright even when we both know it won't. My current method for dealing with stressful days is to hold a pillow in front of my face and scream. Either that or hold it all in until I can go to bed and cry myself to sleep.

I have very few people I consider friends. I'm not interested in being friends with the majority of people I meet. Even when I do find people I can connect with they keep leaving my life for one reason or another. It takes effort to be friends with someone that you aren't conveniently in contact with. I'd be lying if I said I tried my absolute best but how many people can say they've tried that hard?

How many people have randomly called or texted me out of the blue to say "Hey, haven't seen you in a while. How are you doing?" Only one. How many people have messaged me on Facebook for no reason other than to say "Hey buddy. I haven't heard from you in a while. How have things been?" Only two.

I recently had an encounter with a drunk old man who lives in my apartment complex. While he didn't use this word, he basically accused me of having agoraphobia. For those who don't know, that's a fear of going outside. I don't fear the outside world. I just don't desire it. My favorite activities, playing video games, watching anime, writing new songs and stories, can all be done from the comfort of my couch.

I can step outside any time I want. I choose not to leave unless I have a reason. Stepping outside causes me no anxiety it all. It can be a hassle sometimes but so can showering. Are you going to start telling me I have Ablutophobia? For those who haven't heard that word it means a fear of showers.

They say you should live like you were dying. I wouldn't want to jump out of a plane on a normal day. Why would I do it when I know my time is running low? If I know for a fact that my life is about to end, I will do one of two things. Either I'll order a bunch of pizza and marathon through every single anime in existence or I'll put on some music and sit in front of my laptop furiously typing until my fingers fall off. I don't want to leave any of these stories unfinished. I'm betting the majority of people wouldn't be able to figure out the ending I had in mind.

That's why I'm happy I wrote this book. I know it's not the most eloquently told story but at least I got to tell it. This is my life. I deserve to say it in my own words. I didn't write this book to entertain or persuade. This book was written simply to inform. These are the memories I have and this is how I feel about the things that happened to me.

I wanted to make sure you understood exactly what my dream is and why I'm chasing it. I know I've talked about fame enough that some people might have the wrong idea about my true ambitions. I know that at some point in time I'll achieve my goals and someone will say "this is what you asked for." So let's get things straight right now.

I don't want to walk red carpets. I don't want to be on late night talk shows making a fool of myself. I don't want random strangers following me around with cameras trying to create some sort of scandal. I don't want random strangers adoring me. I don't want people I've never met telling me they love me and how much I mean to their lives. I don't want people showing up at my house. That last one has nothing to do with fame. I don't want people at my place period. I need a place in this world that's a haven from the rest of humanity.

I don't want money. I'll take the money of course but not because I desire it. One certainty in life is that there will always be bills to pay. I can guarantee that at some point in time I'll be forced to work on a project I don't believe in because someone put too many zeroes on a check and I'm desperate to stay out of debt. That's why I'm desperate to make it to Hollywood. I'd love the chance to make a living doing something I actually enjoy. Isn't that the American dream?

I wish I was born rich so I could give away every story I've ever written. I love telling stories. I love creating these expansive worlds. I love watching all my characters live their lives. No matter what happens, where my life goes, I'm never going to stop telling my stories. The problem right now is I've got over three hundred stories on my laptop that no one has ever seen. That just doesn't feel right anymore.

I don't want to hear anyone call me brave. I'm not strong either. I'm weak. I didn't survive this long on sheer willpower. It was all luck. Whether that luck was good or bad I have yet to decide. I've given up too many times to be considered strong. I've given up on my dreams. I've given up on life. I'm not chasing my dreams because I'm brave. I'm doing this because I've run out of reasons to wake up in the morning. This dream because is the only thing in this world that I still believe in.

> **"It's down to this.**
> **I've got to make this life make sense."**
> – 3 Doors Down. *Away From The Sun.*

That brings me to my final point. I'm sure most of you are wondering how I chose the title for this book. Every step along the way people have tried to help me in their own way. Many of them giving me the same standard advice again and again. I never took it. Their advice never felt right for me.

There's a quote I try to keep in mind: Everything is impossible until someone does it. When writing this book, I researched the phrase to make sure I didn't get accused of stealing it from someone else. I've seen similar phrases attributed to multiple people. I guess great minds truly do think alike. The first time I heard those words they came out of my own mouth.

When Chris Johnson ran for over 2,000 yards in a single season, I was watching some talking heads on TV discuss whether he, or anyone else, could ever have consecutive 2,000-yard seasons. Someone used the word impossible. That word has always pissed me off. At one point in time human flight was considered impossible. How many humans are soaring through the clouds at this very moment? Impossible is a big word for small minded people.

I know one day I'll make my dreams a reality. Not because I want to…because I need to. No matter how many times I fail I can't stop wanting this. If this book and Toxic don't sell, I already have three other plans in mind. Someway, somehow, I'll find a way to achieve all these life goals that I've set for myself. That's why I chose to title this book: Everything is Impossible. So that when I write the sequel explaining how I made it all work I can give it the title: Until Someone Does It.

"Momma told me never stop
until I bust a nut.
Fuck the world if they can't adjust."
— Tupac Shakur. *Hail Mary*

Everything Is Impossible

Other Books by Nathan Lyle Cunningham

Series #1 | TOXIC – *Before the Beginning*

Series #2 | TOXIC

COMIC BOOK SERIES about Oscar Mireles, a boy from a town that was overrun with radiation. While more than half the town died somehow Oscar was infused with radiation. An accident that took many lives gave Oscar the power to save some. It gave him a great power, but it's also a great curse.

www.ingramcontent.com/pod-product-compliance
Lightning Source LLC
Chambersburg PA
CBHW071350290426
44108CB00014B/1491